Current
CONTROVERSIES

The Dark Web

Other Books in the Current Controversies Series

The Dark Web

Eamon Doyle, Book Editor

GREENHAVEN
PUBLISHING

Published in 2020 by Greenhaven Publishing, LLC
353 3rd Avenue, Suite 255, New York, NY 10010

Copyright © 2020 by Greenhaven Publishing, LLC

First Edition

Articles in Greenhaven Publishing anthologies are often edited for length to meet page
requirements. In addition, original titles of these works are changed to clearly present
the main thesis and to explicitly indicate the author's opinion. Every effort is made to
ensure that Greenhaven Publishing accurately reflects the original intent of the authors.
Every effort has been made to trace the owners of the copyrighted material.

Cover image: picture alliance/Getty Images

Cataloging-in-Publication Data

Names: Doyle, Eamon, editor.
Title: The dark web / Eamon Doyle, book editor.
Description: New York : Greenhaven Publishing, 2020. | Series: Current controversies
| Includes bibliographical references and index. | Audience: Grades 9-12.
Identifiers: ISBN 9781534506077 (library binding) | ISBN 9781534506060 (paperback)
Subjects: LCSH: Computer crimes. | Dark Web. | Internet. | World Wide Web.
Classification: LCC HV6773.D375 2020 | DDC 364.16'8—dc23

Manufactured in the United States of America

Website: http://greenhavenpublishing.com

Contents

Dr. Kat Hadjimatheou outlines a number of areas in which law enforcement surveillance of activity on the dark web can be ethically problematic. In particular, she focuses on the risks of inadvertently criminalizing innocent activities and the use of new and unorthodox surveillance techniques.

Chapter 2: Is It Possible to Effectively Monitor and Regulate Activity on the Dark Web?

Yes: It Is Possible to Provide Adequate Oversight of Dark Web Activity

Jacob Koshy

Koshy, an expert on big data marketing and web technology, argues that techniques such as "web crawling"—which was originally developed for private sector use—could be applied in a law enforcement context to more effectively monitor the dark web universe.

Katie A. Paul

In this viewpoint, Katie A. Paul looks at the various ways in which criminal and terrorist groups have utilized the art and antiquities market on the dark web to launder money and conceal financial transactions. She argues that widespread use of the dark web by nefarious actors should be viewed as a surveillance opportunity for law enforcement agencies.

Shawn R. Kehoe

The dark web has expanded in recent years, and it is up to law enforcement professionals to find ways to patrol it. This would involve increasing the resources available for cyber monitoring and improving technical training for law enforcement officers.

Europol

In 2017, two of the largest criminal dark web markets—AlphaBay and Hansa—were taken down through coordinated law enforcement operations by the FBI, DEA, Dutch National Police, and Europol. Despite the anonymous and elusive nature of the dark web, this suggests that it is possible to hold the criminals who use it accountable.

No: The Networks That Make Up the Dark Web Are Too Nebulous to Fully Monitor

Chapter 3: Are There Safe and Legitimate Uses for the Dark Web?

Yes: There Are Uses for the Dark Web and Its Anonymity Beyond Criminal Activities

This viewpoint delves into the world of crypto-markets and underlines the reasons why participants should take appropriate security precautions when engaging in "dark" transactions.

No: The Dark Web Will Always Be an Inherent Security Risk That Benefits Criminals

to an increased level of risk and volatility in most cryptocurrency investments.

Pierluigi Paganini

The author, who is a cyber security analyst with over twenty years of experience, explains how the dark web environment works to criminals' advantage as they work to conceal their activities from law enforcement scrutiny.

Europol

It is crucial that the black market operating on the dark web be brought under control, which is why Europol established a dedicated dark web team to combat it in the European Union. Other nations and regions must follow suit in order to reduce criminal activity on the dark web.

Foreword

"Controversy" is a word that has an undeniably unpleasant connotation. It carries a definite negative charge. Controversy can spoil family gatherings, spread a chill around classroom and campus discussion, inflame public discourse, open raw civic wounds, and lead to the ouster of public officials. We often feel that controversy is almost akin to bad manners, a rude and shocking eruption of that which must not be spoken or thought of in polite, tightly guarded society. To avoid controversy, to quell controversy, is often seen as a public good, a victory for etiquette, perhaps even a moral or ethical imperative.

Yet the studious, deliberate avoidance of controversy is also a whitewashing, a denial, a death threat to democracy. It is a false sterilizing and sanitizing and superficial ordering of the messy, ragged, chaotic, at times ugly processes by which a healthy democracy identifies and confronts challenges, engages in passionate debate about appropriate approaches and solutions, and arrives at something like a consensus and a broadly accepted and supported way forward. Controversy is the megaphone, the speaker's corner, the public square through which the citizenry finds and uses its voice. Controversy is the life's blood of our democracy and absolutely essential to the vibrant health of our society.

Our present age is certainly no stranger to controversy. We are consumed by fierce debates about technology, privacy, political correctness, poverty, violence, crime and policing, guns, immigration, civil and human rights, terrorism, militarism, environmental protection, and gender and racial equality. Loudly competing voices are raised every day, shouting opposing opinions, putting forth competing agendas, and summoning starkly different visions of a utopian or dystopian future. Often these voices attempt to shout the others down; there is precious little listening and considering among the cacophonous din. Yet listening and considering, too, are essential to the health of a democracy. If controversy is democracy's lusty lifeblood, respectful listening and careful thought are its higher faculties, its brain, its conscience.

Current Controversies does not shy away from or attempt to hush the loudly competing voices. It seeks to provide readers with as wide and representative as possible a range of articulate voices on any given controversy of the day, separates each one out to allow it to be heard clearly and fairly, and encourages careful listening to each of these well-crafted, thoughtfully expressed opinions, supplied by some of today's leading academics, thinkers, analysts, politicians, policy makers, economists, activists, change agents, and advocates. Only after listening to a wide range of opinions on an issue, evaluating the strengths and weaknesses of each argument, assessing how well the facts and available evidence mesh with the stated opinions and conclusions, and thoughtfully and critically examining one's own beliefs and conscience can the reader begin to arrive at his or her own conclusions and articulate his or her own stance on the spotlighted controversy.

This process is facilitated and supported in each Current Controversies volume by an introduction and chapter overviews that provide readers with the essential context they need to begin engaging with the spotlighted controversies, with the debates surrounding them, and with their own perhaps shifting or nascent opinions on them. Chapters are organized around several key questions that are answered with diverse opinions representing all points on the political spectrum. In its content, organization, and methodology, readers are encouraged to determine the authors' point of view and purpose, interrogate and analyze the various arguments and their rhetoric and structure, evaluate the arguments' strengths and weaknesses, test their claims against available facts and evidence, judge the validity of the reasoning, and bring into clearer, sharper focus the reader's own beliefs and conclusions and how they may differ from or align with those in the collection or those of classmates.

Research has shown that reading comprehension skills improve dramatically when students are provided with compelling, intriguing, and relevant "discussable" texts. The subject matter of these collections could not be more compelling, intriguing, or urgently relevant to today's students and the world they are poised to inherit. The anthologized articles also provide the basis for stimulating, lively, and passionate classroom debates. Students who are compelled to anticipate objections to their own argument and identify the flaws in those of an opponent read more carefully, think more critically, and steep themselves in relevant context, facts, and information more thoroughly. In short, using discussable text of the kind provided by every single volume in the Current Controversies series encourages close reading, facilitates reading comprehension, fosters research, strengthens critical thinking, and greatly enlivens and energizes classroom discussion and participation. The entire learning process is deepened, extended, and strengthened.

If we are to foster a knowledgeable, responsible, active, and engaged citizenry, we must provide readers with the intellectual, interpretive, and critical-thinking tools and experience necessary to make sense of the world around them and of the all-important debates and arguments that inform it. We must encourage them not to run away from or attempt to quell controversy but to embrace it in a responsible, conscientious, and thoughtful way, to sharpen and strengthen their own informed opinions by listening to and critically analyzing those of others. This series encourages respectful engagement with and analysis of current controversies and competing opinions and fosters a resulting increase in the strength and rigor of one's own opinions and stances. As such, it helps readers assume their rightful place in the public square and provides them with the skills necessary to uphold their awesome responsibility—guaranteeing the continued and future health of a vital, vibrant, and free democracy.

Introduction

"The dark net is a world of power and freedom: of expression, of creativity, of information, of ideas. Power and freedom endow our creative and our destructive faculties. The dark net magnifies both, making it easier to explore every desire, to act on every dark impulse, to indulge every neurosis."

—Jamie Bartlett, British author and journalist

Changes and advancements in the technology of information— such as the arrival of the printing press, the birth of industrial capitalism, and the introduction of the radio, television, and home computer—catalyzed many of the major political, cultural, and economic trends of the last six centuries and laid the groundwork for what we recognize as modern life. Over the last three decades, this pattern has continued with the advent of internet technology, cryptocurrency, hacker culture, social media, and the looming specter of cyber warfare. Although it is surely among the most prominent features of modern life, the internet also happens to be one of the most poorly understood.

The mainstream, surface-level internet that most casual users are familiar with—the world of .com sites, standard search engines, non-encrypted data, and so on—comprises only a tiny percentage of the actual data space on the web. The remaining parts are known as the *deep web* and the *dark web*. The deep web refers to all of the remaining content, which is distinguished by its independence from search engine indexing systems. The dark web refers to a specific subset of encrypted material that is accessible only with special software, the most common example of which is an encrypted internet browser known as The Onion Router (TOR).

It is difficult to generalize about the range of activities that take place on dark web networks. Internet technology expert Dr. Kat Hadjimatheou explains:

> While there is nothing ethically or legally dubious about encryption in principle, the reality is that much of the activity on the Dark Web by people in liberal democracies is unethical and/or illegal. The Dark Web hosts a vast range of sites and forums for unethical and illegal behaviour, from illicit markets for drugs, counterfeit goods, and contract killings to money laundering, extremist sites and forums for the sharing of child sexual abuse material. All of these activities are legitimate targets of policing, and all are made easier to perform and more difficult to prevent and prosecute by encryption. However, it is not only criminals who use the dark net. Political dissidents and activists, journalists, law enforcement and the military also take advantage of the security and anonymity offered by encryption.[1]

In recent years, growing awareness of the dark web and its resources has prompted questions, discussion, and considerable controversy around the world. Opinions generally fall into two categories: those who view its resources in terms of freedom of speech and information tend to emphasize its positive qualities, whereas those who view it in terms of cybersecurity tend to worry about its risks.

Those who advocate for dark web users often cite examples where journalists, political dissidents, and human rights advocates have used encrypted networks when operating in hostile, totalitarian political environments. The technology writer Summer Lightfoot argues:

> Although the deep web certainly has its dark parts, it also has some incredibly beneficial uses. Reformers and political

dissidents around the world use the dark web to communicate and build movements for deserving and lawful protest and reform in war-torn areas such as Syria. Tor's early adopters weren't criminals, they were dissidents.[2]

On the other hand, law enforcement and intelligence professionals have pointed out that the encrypted, anonymous nature of dark web activity makes it an ideal environment for criminals and other nefarious actors.

For many years, the TOR network hosted an online market for illegal drugs known as the Silk Road, and although its founder and organizer—hacker Ross William Ulbricht, better known by his online moniker Dread Pirate Roberts—was eventually arrested and jailed, similar markets emerged almost immediately. Terrorist organizations including ISIS and al-Qaeda have also utilized dark web technology to communicate and to conceal financial transactions. The market intelligence manager Michelle Bovée writes:

> The dark web is everywhere, intertwined with everything from international terrorism to global activist movements to ordinary, confidential web access. This means, for better or worse, policymakers and international organizations are going to have to figure out how to cope with this wild west of the Internet, how to trace and prevent illegal activity while preserving the secure elements used by reporters and activists alike.[3]

Clearly it is a space that demands the attention of law enforcement and security professionals. But that is no easy task, given the delicate ethical and political issues at stake when the flow of information is subject to regulation. Former US Secretary of Homeland Security Michael Chertoff writes:

> Creating policy to address the Dark Web requires an understanding of the benefits and risks of anonymity and of an open internet. Rash and sweeping legislation has the potential to encroach on civil liberties and to be a nightmare to enforce. On the other hand, not addressing the Dark Web will allow illicit activities to persist unabated. It is impossible to regulate

the Dark Web in isolation; any regulations must be applicable to the internet as a whole and will thus affect Surface Web users, Deep Web researchers, and Dark Web criminals alike.[4]

The challenges that Chertoff describes will play a major role in determining the political environment of the future. Indeed, political scientists distinguish democratic systems from authoritarian ones largely on the basis of how information technology and media ecosystems are regulated. In theory, democratic government calls for open, free-flowing channels of distribution to ensure widespread access among citizens who need reliable information in order to perform their basic role in the system. Authoritarian governance, on the other hand, generally entails rigid controls on the public distribution of information.

Current Controversies: The Dark Web provides perspectives from experts in finance, technology, law enforcement, government, and various other fields on the potential and actualized risks and rewards of the dark web. Whether we like it or not, the dark web has become a central part of the modern world, and it is up to us to answer the fundamentally political question of how to deal with it. The stakes could hardly be any higher.

Notes

1. "Policing the Dark Web: Ethical and Legal Issues," by Kat Hadjimatheou, MEDI@4SEC. Reprinted by permission.

2. "Surveillance and Privacy on the Deep Web," by Summer Lightfoot, May 5, 2017. Reprinted by permission.

3. "International Relations in the Dark," by Michelle Bovée, Charged Affairs, March 23, 2016. Reprinted by permission.

4. "A Public Policy Perspective of the Dark Web," by Michael Chertoff, *Journal of Cyber Policy*, Taylor & Francis, March 13, 2017. Reprinted by permission.

CHAPTER 1

Do the Dark Web's Security Risks Outweigh the Ethical Issues of Policing It?

The Dark Web Is a World of Its Own

Davey Winder

Davey Winder is a journalist and consultant who specializes in information technology and cybersecurity issues. His writing has appeared in Forbes, Infosecurity Magazine, *and the* Sunday Times. *He was named BT Security Journalist of the Year in 2006, 2008, and 2010.*

The Dark Web is an online community accessed by groups with a range of agendas that want to protect their anonymity—whether this be online criminals, activists or those wishing simply to maintain their online privacy."

These are the words of Rik Ferguson, vice president of security research at Trend Micro and a special adviser to European Union law enforcement agency Europol.

When he investigated the Dark Web he found that light drugs were one of the most traded items, with hard drugs, pirated games and stolen accounts alongside. "Many Dark Web users, or at least those who frequent the top marketplace, go there to purchase illicit drugs," he says. But what, exactly, is the Dark Web?

What Is Dark Web?

Invisible to search engines such as Google, the Dark Web is made possible by darknets—networks which can only be accessed with specific software and authorisation—through networks where connections are made between trusted peers.

The best known, and by far the most popular, darknet is the Onion Router (Tor), which was created by the US Naval Research Labs in the 90s as an enabler of secure communication and funded by the US Department of Defense. To navigate it you use the Tor browser, similar to Google Chrome or Internet Explorer apart from

"Delving into the World of the Dark Web," by Davey Winder, Raconteur Media Ltd, March 8, 2016. Reprinted by permission.

keeping the identity of the person doing the browsing a secret. Importantly, this secrecy also applies to what the user is looking at.

It is because servers hosting websites on the Tor network, denoted by their .onion (dot onion) designation, are able to mask their location, originally to enable government dropsites and information silos to exist without trace, that when Tor software went public in 2003, the Dark Web became a reality.

This combination of hidden servers and anonymous users enables a .onion version of Facebook for those who fear being spied upon, and empowers political activists to continue protests while protected from regimes that would take away more than their liberty. Unfortunately, Tor is also used by the criminal fraternity as a dark marketplace.

Using a crawler bot that scraped the .onion sites accessible to it, researchers at King's College London recently attempted to map criminal activity on the Dark Web. The results suggested some 57 per cent of Tor sites host illegal content. What the study didn't find was evidence of Islamic extremism, claiming a near absence of jihadi activity.

Indeed, that around 40 per cent of the crawled Tor activity does not fall under the label of criminal endeavour reveals the dichotomy of the Dark Web; it treads the line between being a saviour of free speech and a criminal marketplace of the most extreme kind.

Perhaps the best known example of a dark market was Silk Road. Shut down in 2013 after an FBI sting operation, which would eventually see its creator, Ross Ulbricht aka Dread Pirate Roberts, jailed for life, Silk Road was like an eBay of criminality. The closure of Silk Road has not meant that criminal activity on the Dark Web has shut up shop alongside it, however.

"Today, anything and everything is available on the Dark Web from guns and explosives to designer drugs and paedophile material, from hacking code to identities and credit cards," says Andrew Beckett, managing director at security intelligence specialists Kroll. "What is more surprising is the growth of online services and support around these activities, and the way they are run as big businesses."

While five years ago you could buy a DDoS (distributed denial-of-service) attack to take down a site of your choosing for around £35 per day, now that has dropped to £20. This is what has become known as Cybercrime-as-a-Service (CaaS) and those wishing to create a sophisticated attack are spoilt for choice on the Dark Web.

Law Enforcement Changing the Scene

But have successful law enforcement investigations, such as the Silk Road case, changed the Dark Web operationally?

"It is only natural for criminals to become more suspecting and hesitant, for malware vendors to disappear and for the expert-level fraudsters to go deeper underground after a major bust," says Limor Kessem, senior cyber security evangelist at IBM Security and a Dark Web expert.

Ms Kessem has witnessed the gradual departure of banking Trojan developers from the Dark Web as they realised just how dangerous their activity was and how some of the best-known developers were being arrested. Anyone wanting to access the more "elite" marketplaces on the Dark Web will not only have to know precisely how to reach them, but also need to know someone within the community who can vouch for them and possibly pay a joining fee.

"In some cases they have to prove that they are criminals or show their 'work' in some way," she says, concluding that for everyday folk or criminal chancers these boards are almost impossible to join.

Assuming you are among the criminal fraternity with access to Dark Web markets, what are the trading tools that are considered essential for doing business in the shadows of the internet?

A Tor browser is something of a given, however most serious criminals will ensure the devices they access the Dark Web from remain free of as many traceable artefacts as possible.

"Most will utilise USB bootable operating systems such as 'Tails' to make sure that nothing is saved to their hard disks," says Adam Tyler, chief innovation officer at security specialists CSID. "Tails is a Linux-based OS [operating system] that can be started on pretty much any computer and forces all internet connections through Tor, while encrypting all files and e-mails, and leaving no traces on the host device. Most payments are made using bitcoin, but the career criminals know better than to use it without proper precautions.

"Due to an ability to connect links between addresses and identities, many choose to utilise 'bitcoin tumblers' to attempt to evade identification or association." Tumblers effectively launder the currency by a user transferring their bitcoin into a tumble pool and then withdrawing a collection of unrelated coins to the same value.

As Kroll's Mr Beckett concludes: "The expansion of the Dark Web looks set to continue as criminals find evermore innovative ways to monetise their activities and offer them as a service. The ability to hide this activity from law enforcement and to mask the financial transactions by using bitcoin or bartering only increases the attractiveness."

Dark Web Shopping List of Crime

Credit Cards (£3-£10 Each)
Credit cards remain easy to buy on the Dark Web with US-based cards available for £3 each, while EU and UK cards are more sought after and can be sold for three times as much. A premium is placed upon card data guaranteed not reported stolen at the time of sale.

Infected Computers (£15 per 1,000)
A sad reflection of how easy it is to infect a computer and turn it into a "bot" which can then be used as part of a botnet to launch DDoS attacks for example, is how cheap they are being sold. The more you buy, the cheaper they get with 10,000 bots going for £100.

Loyalty Accounts (£15-£1,000)
There is increased buying interest for loyalty accounts that can be used by criminals to pursue profitable social engineering attacks. Hotel loyalty account data can sell for as little as £15, while eBay profiles with a very high reputation status can reach as much as £1,000.

Recreational Drugs (£25+)
Although the ill-fated Silk Road was the best known illegal drugs marketplace on the Dark Web, the deals have not stopped since its demise. Recent research reveals average prices of £70 per gram of cocaine, MDMA at £25 a gram and ten tabs of acid for £75.

Hackers for Hire (from £100)
If you look hard enough you will find hackers, complete with customer feedback ratings, offering services from as little as £100 for hacking an e-mail account up to £500 or more for corporate espionage, reputational damage and so on.

US Citizenship (£4,000)
The option to "become a US citizen" is provided in a package, containing a passport, social security number, driving licence and birth certificate, can be bought, along with supporting documentation. Fake passports are sold separately for £650 and counterfeit driving licences are £150.

Handguns (£450)
Perhaps surprisingly, not a US-only market. Handguns are being traded within Europe and can be purchased with prices starting from £450. Delivery might be problematical though, even with promises of weapons being stripped and dispatched in pieces.

Assassins for Hire (£25,000 upwards)

Yes, you can even rent the services of a hitman on the Dark Web. Sellers of such services require the bitcoin fees to be placed into escrow and, once the hit has been carried out, the funds are released. Don't expect much in the way of references or customer feedback.

Dark Web Terrorism Is a Serious Threat

Gabriel Weimann

Gabriel Weimann is a professor of communications at the University of Haifa in Israel and a former fellow at the Woodrow Wilson International Center for Scholars.

Beneath the familiar online world that most of us know and use, a world of *YouTube, Google, Facebook*, and *Twitter*, lies a hidden network of sites, communities, and platforms where people can be anyone, or do anything they want. This is the Dark Web. One can describe the Internet as composed of layers: the "upper" layer, or the Surface Web, can easily be accessed by regular searches or directing your web browser to a known website address. However, "deeper" layers, the content of the Deep Web, are not indexed by traditional search engines such as Google. The deepest layers of the Deep Web, a segment known as the "Dark Web," contain content that has been intentionally concealed. The Dark Web can be defined as the portion of the Deep Web that can only be accessed through specialized browsers. A recent study found that 57% of the Dark Web is occupied by illegal content like pornography, illicit finances, drug hubs, weapons trafficking, counterfeit currency, terrorist communication, and much more.[1] Probably the most notorious example of these activities can be seen in The Silk Road website. In October 2013, the FBI shut down the first version of this drug market and arrested its owner Ross William Ulbricht. The Dark Web has been associated with the infamous WikiLeaks, as well as Bitcoin, said to be the currency of the Dark Web. Over its successful two-year run, The Silk Road made over US $1.2 billion in bitcoins. Of course, dissident political groups, civil rights activists and investigative journalists in oppressive countries

"Terrorist Migration to the Dark Web," by Gabriel Weimann, Terrorism Research Initiative, June 2016. http://www.terrorismanalysts.com/pt/index.php/pot/article/view/513/html. Licensed under CC BY 3.0 Unported.

have also been known to use the Dark Web to communicate and organize clandestinely.

To access material in the Dark Web, individuals use special software such as TOR (The Onion Router) or I2P (Invisible Internet Project). TOR was initially created by the US Naval Research Laboratory as a tool for anonymously communicating online. It relies upon a network of volunteer computers to route users' web traffic through a series of other users' computers so that the traffic cannot be traced to the original user. Not all Dark Web sites use TOR (i.e., ".onion") addresses, but a TOR-enabled web browser can access virtually any site without revealing the user's identity. On the Dark Web, a visitor must know where to find the site in order to access it. A few search engines have been developed for the Dark Web, but they are limited in scope and usefulness.

Terrorist Interest in the Dark Web

Terrorists have been active on various online platforms since the late 1990s.[2] However, the Surface Web was discovered to be too risky for anonymity-seeking terrorists: they could be monitored, traced and found. Many of the terrorist websites and social media on the Surface Web are monitored by counter-terrorism agencies and are often shut down or hacked. In contrast, on the Dark Web, decentralized and anonymous networks enable evading arrest and the closure of these terrorist platforms. According to the London-based *Quilliam Foundation*, "The terrorist material reappears on the Internet as quickly as it is banished and this policy risks driving fanatics on to the 'dark web' where they are even harder to track." Moreover, "Islamist forums and chat rooms in English and French are still widely available, but...a large portion of more extremist Islamic discourse now takes place within the dark web."[3] "ISIL's activities on the Surface Web are now being monitored closely, and the decision by a number of governments to take down or filter extremist content has forced the jihadists to look for new online safe havens," Berton writes in her report on ISIS's use of the Dark Web.[4]

Following the November 2015 attacks in Paris, ISIS has turned to the Dark Web to spread news and propaganda in an apparent attempt to protect the identities of the group's supporters and safeguard its content from hacktivists. The move comes after hundreds of websites associated with ISIS were taken down as part of the *Operation Paris* (OpParis) campaign launched by the amorphous hacker collective Anonymous. ISIS's media outlet, *Al-Hayat Media Center*, posted a link and explanations on how to get to their new Dark Web site on a forum associated with ISIS. The announcement was also distributed on *Telegram*, the encrypted communication application used by the group. *Telegram* is an application for sending text and multimedia messages on Android, iOS, and Windows devices. *Telegram* is so confident of its security that it twice offered a $300,000 reward to the first person who could crack its encryption. The messages shared links to a Tor service with a ".onion" address on the Dark Web. The site contains an archive of ISIS propaganda materials, including its documentary-style film, *The Flames of War*. The site also includes a link to the terrorist group's private messaging portal on *Telegram*. My earlier report on terrorists' use of the Dark Web revealed some early indications of the growing terrorist interest in the dark online platforms.[5] However, within several months, monitoring of online terrorism added new indications, new findings and new trends of terrorist presence in the Dark Web.

What Are Terrorists Doing on the Dark Web?

A simple description of what terrorists do on the Dark Web would be, "more of the same but more secretly." However, that is only partially true. Terrorists are using the Dark Web as they have been using the Surface Web for several decades, but there are also new opportunities offered now to cyber-savvy operatives. Terrorists have used the Internet to provide information to fellow terrorists, to recruit and radicalize, to spread propaganda, to raise funds, and to coordinate actions and attacks. All of this activity, however, has now shifted to deeper layers of the Internet. Terrorist propaganda material, for example, is now stowed in the Dark Web. On 15 November 2015, two days after the Paris attacks, ISIS posted a message discussing their official *Isdarat* website, which archives propaganda and releases. The message contained links to a hidden Tor service with a ".onion" address, indicating the move of the *Isdarat* outlet to the Dark Web. The message declared: "Due to severe constraints imposed on the #*Caliphate*_Publications website, any new domain is deleted after being posted. We announce the launch of the website for "dark web." The online libraries of terrorist material led several Jihadists to suggest a "Jihadwiki".[6] In December 2015 an al-Qaeda group called the "al-Aqsa IT Team" distributed a manual entitled "Tor Browser Security Guidelines" for ensuring online anonymity while using Tor software. It offers step-by-step instructions for everything from downloading and installing the browser to steps for hindering geolocation and identification by counter-terrorism agencies.

Terrorists are now using the Dark Web also to communicate in a safer way than ever before. Although it has been long assumed that terrorist attacks are coordinated in a secret network, solid evidence has only been attained in 2013. In August 2013, the US National Security Agency (NSA) intercepted encrypted communications between al-Qaeda leader Ayman Al-Zawahiri and Nasir Al-Wuhaysi, the head of the Yemen-based al-Qaeda in the Arabian Peninsula. The Institute for National Security Studies revealed that, for about a decade, the communication between leaders of the worldwide al-Qaeda network "apparently took place in a part of the Internet sometimes called deepnet, blacknet, or darknet."[7]

Recently, ISIS and other jihadist groups have used new online applications which allow users to broadcast their messages to an unlimited number of members via encrypted mobile phone apps such as *Telegram*. Since it went live on 14 August 2013, *Telegram* has seen major success, both among ordinary users as well as terrorists. But it was not until its launch of "channels" in September 2015 that the Terrorism Research & Analysis Consortium (TRAC) began to witness a massive migration from other social media sites, most notably *Twitter*, to *Telegram*.[8] On 26 September 2015, just four days after *Telegram* rolled out channels, ISIS media operatives on *Twitter* started advertising the group's own channel dubbed *Nashir*, which translates to "Distributor" in English. A recent ICT special report on *Telegram* revealed that "since September 2015, we have witnessed a significant increase in the use of the *Telegram* software (software for sending encrypted instant messages) by the Islamic State and al-Qaeda. In March 2016 alone, 700 new channels identified with the Islamic State were opened".[9]

While many of the channels have Islamic State affiliations, there are an increasing number of channels from other major players in the global jihadi world: these include al-Qaeda in the Arabian Peninsula (AQAP), Ansar al-Sharia in Libya (ASL) and Jabhat al-Nusra (JN) and Jaysh al-Islam, both in Syria. Al-Qaeda's Yemeni branch (AQAP) launched its own *Telegram* channel on 25 September 2015 and the Libyan Ansar al-Shari'ah group created its channel the following day. According to a TRAC report, membership growth for each discrete channel is staggering. Within a week's time, one single Islamic State channel went from 5,000 members to well over 10,000.[10] When asked about it, *Telegram*'s CEO Pavel Durov conceded that ISIS indeed uses *Telegram* to ensure the security of its communications, but added: "I think that privacy, ultimately, and our right for privacy is more important than our fear of bad things happening, like terrorism."[11]

Another safe communication application adapted by terrorists is the *TrueCrypt*. One of the ISIS members who was captured by French police in August 2015 revealed details about this program. Reda Hame, a Parisian IT specialist who traveled to Syria to join ISIS and fight was instead put through a rapid training course and sent back to France to carry out an attack. Hame provided details of his training to use *TrueCrypt*, an encryption application, and how, before returning to France, he was given a USB drive containing the program. The ISIS technicians also instructed Hame to transfer *TrueCrypt* from the USB key to a second computer once he reached Europe. *TrueCrypt* was launched in 2004 by Paul Le Roux, a programmer and a crime lord, who operated a global drug, arms and money-laundering cartel out of a base in the Philippines. Le Roux was arrested in Liberia on drug-trafficking charges in September 2012. But *TrueCrypt* is still active and backdoor-free, which explains why ISIS terrorists still use it for encrypted communications and file sharing.

Terrorists can use the Dark Web for fundraising, money transfers, and illegal purchase of explosives and weapons, using virtual currencies like Bitcoin and other crypto-currencies. For instance, "Fund the Islamic Struggle without Leaving a Trace" is a Deep Web page which invites donations for Jihad through transactions to a particular Bitcoin address. A PDF document posted online under the pseudonym of Amreeki Witness titled "Bitcoin wa Sadaqat alJihad," which translates to "Bitcoin and the Charity of Violent Physical Struggle," is in fact a guide for using the Dark Web for secretive financial transactions.[12] The weapons used for the deadly Paris attacks are now thought to have been purchased from a hidden Dark Web store, which, according to official documents from the Stuttgart prosecutor's office, was a German Dark Net vendor under the username DW Guns.[13] Some reports revealed that the Dark Web has also become a medium for some terrorist organizations to sell on online black markets human organs (probably of their captives), as well as stolen oil or smuggled antiquities looted from ancient cities.[14]

In January 2015, the Singapore-based cyber intelligence company S2T uncovered concrete evidence that a terror cell, purporting to be related to Islamic State and operating in the Americas, is soliciting Bitcoin as part of its fundraising efforts. [15] The online message from the group's fundraiser, a man later identified only as Abu-Mustafa, declared: "One cannot send a bank transfer to a mujahid [someone engaged in Jihad] or suspected mujahid without the kafir [infidel] governments ruling today immediately being aware…A proposed solution to this is something known as Bitcoin …To set up a totally anonymous donation system that could send millions of dollars' worth of Bitcoin instantly…right to the pockets of the mujahideen, very little would be done [against it]."[16] Another example comes from Indonesia where a Jihadist group collected donations, both from national and international donors, through Bitcoins on the Dark Web. Furthermore, getting a stolen identity from the Dark Web, they hacked a Forex trading website to whip the points of the member. From these series of cybercrimes, the terrorist group collected US $600,000.[17]

The Challenge of Dark Web Terrorism

Terrorists flying drones to spread highly radioactive material over a civilian area: this is part of the nightmare scenario that US President Barack Obama urged world leaders to consider as they debated better ways of controlling nuclear material. Speaking to a group of 50 heads of state and foreign ministers in Washington, D.C., in April 2016, President Obama described how a terrorist group had bought isotopes through brokers on the Dark Web. In March 2016, the French Interior Minister, Bernard Cazeneuve, argued that the Dark Web is being used extensively by terrorists. In a meeting of the National Assembly, he said that those who have been responsible for the recent terrorist strikes in Europe have been making use of the deep web, communicating through encrypted messages.

The growing sophistication of terrorists' use of the Dark Web presents a tough challenge for governments, counter-terrorism agencies, and security services. There is an urgent need to develop new methods and measures for tracking and analyzing terrorist use of the Dark Web. Thus, for example, the American Defense Advanced Research Projects Agency (DARPA) believes the answer can be found in MEMEX, a software that allows for better cataloguing of Deep Web sites. Providing clear evidence that shows the Dark Web has turned into a major platform for global terrorism and criminal activities is absolutely crucial in order to provide the impetus for the necessary tools to be developed to counter it. MEMEX was originally developed for monitoring human trafficking on the Deep Web; but the same principles can be applied to almost any illicit Deep Web activity. In February 2015, a special report entitled "The Impact of the Dark Web on Internet Governance and Cyber Security" presented several suggestions regarding the Dark Web.[18] The report states that "in order to formulate comprehensive strategies and policies for governing the Internet, it is important to consider insights on its farthest reaches—the Deep Web and, more importantly, the Dark Web." It also notes that "While the Dark Web may lack the broad appeal that is available on the Surface Web, the hidden ecosystem is conducive for propaganda, recruitment, financing and planning, which relates to our original understanding of the Dark Web as an unregulated space."

Finally, it is necessary to remember that the Dark Web also serves journalists, civil rights advocates, and democracy activists—all of whom may be under threat of censorship or imprisonment. Thus, the alarming infiltration of Internet-savvy terrorists to the "virtual caves" of the Dark Web should trigger an international search for a solution to combat illegal and nefarious activities, but one that should not impair legitimate, lawful freedom of expression.

Notes

[1] Moore, Daniel. & Rid, Thomas. 2016. "Cryptopolitik and the Darknet", *Survival*, 58:1, 7-38. Accessed April 30, 2016; URL: http://www.tandfonline.com/doi/full/10.1080/00396338.2016.1142085.

[2] Weimann, Gabriel. 2006. *Terror on the Internet*. Washington, D.C.: United States Institute of Peace; Weimann, G. 2015. *Terrorism in Cyberspace: The Next Generation*. New York: Columbia University Press.

[3] Hussain, Ghaffar and Saltman, Erin Marie, 2014. "Jihad Trending: A Comprehensive Analysis of Online Extremism and How to Counter It". A special report by *Quilliam*, May 2014; accessed October 1, 2015.URL: http://www.quilliamfoundation.org/wp/wp-content/uploads/publications/free/jihad-trending-quilliam.

[4] Berton, Beatrice, 2015. "The dark side of the web: ISIL's one-stop shop?". Report of the European Union Institute for Security Studies, June 2015 accessed March 1,

2016. URL:http://www.iss.europa.eu/uploads/media/Alert_30_The_Dark_Web. pdf .

[5] Weimann, Gabriel, 2016. "Going Dark: Terrorism on the Dark Web", *Studies in Conflict & Terrorism* 39, 195-206. URL: http://www.tandfonline.com/doi/abs/10.1 080/1057610X.2015.1119546.

[6] SITE Intelligence Group. 2014. "Jihadist Suggests Creating "Jihadwiki."" URL: https://news.siteintelgroup.com/Jihadist-News/jihadist-suggests-creating-qjihadwikiq.html.

[7] The Institute for National Security Studies (INSS), 2013. "Backdoor Plots: The Darknet as a Field for Terrorism", September 10, 2013.URL: http://www.inss.org.il/ index.aspx?id=4538&articleid=5574.

[8] TRAC. 2015. "Massive Migration to Telegram, the New Jihadist Destination", *TRAC Insight*, November 4, 2015.URL: http://www. trackingterrorism.org/chatter/trac-insight-massive-migration-telegram-new-jihadist-destination.

[9] International Center for Counter-Terrorism (ICT), 2016. "The Telegram Chat Software as an Arena of Activity to Encourage the 'Lone Wolf' Phenomenon", May 24, 2016. URL: https://www.ict.org.il/Article/1673/the-telegram-chat-software-as-an-arena-of-activity-to-encourage-the-lone-wolf-phenomenon.

[10] TRAC. 2015. "Massive Migration to Telegram, the new Jihadist Destination", op. cit.

[11] Cited in the *Washington Post*, November 19, 2015.URL: https://www. washingtonpost.com/news/morning-mix/wp/2015/11/19/founder-of-app-used-by-isis-once-said-we-shouldnt-feel-guilty-on-wednesday-he-banned-their-accounts/.

[12] The document is available online; URL: https://alkhilafaharidat.files.wordpress. com/2014/07/btcedit-21.pdf.

[13] Reported in numerous news outlets. See, for example, *Fox News*. URL: http:// www.foxnews.com/world/2015/11/27/germany-arrests-man-reportedly-suspected-selling-guns-to-paris-attackers.html.

[14] Wimmer, Andreas and Nastiti, Aulia, 2015. "Darknet, Social Media, and Extremism: Addressing Indonesian Counterterrorism on the Internet", *Deutsches Asienforschungszentrum Asian Series Commentaries*, Vol. 30. URL:https://www. academia.edu/20813843/DARKNET_SOCIAL_MEDIA_AND_EXTREMISM_ ADDRESSING_INDONESIAN_COUNTERTERRORISM_ON_THE_ INTERNET.

[15] "U.S.-based ISIS Cell Fundraising on the Dark Web, New Evidence Suggests", *Haaretz*, January 29, 2015; URL: http://www.haaretz.com/middle-east-news/.premium-1.639542.

[16] Cited in "Supporter of Extremist Group ISIS Explains How Bitcoin Could Be Used To Fund Jihad", *Business Insider,* July 8, 2014; URL: http://www. businessinsider.com/isis-supporter-outlines-how-to-support-terror-group-with-bitcoin-2014-7.

[17] Wimmer and Nastiti, 2015, op. cit.

[18] Chertoff, Michael and Simon, Tobby. 2015. "The Impact of the Dark Web on Internet Governance and Cyber Security"; URL: https://www.cigionline.org/sites/default/files/gcig_paper_no6.pdf.

Cryptocurrency Enables Financial Crime

Simone D. Casadei Bernardi

Simone D. Casadei Bernardi is a writer, consultant, and managing director and CAO at European Business Advisory Limited. He specializes in financial technology and associated regulatory issues.

Criminals see cryptoassets as the perfect medium for financial crime. That's because of the perceived anonymity a person enjoys when they use Bitcoin and similar currencies. But is there proof that cryptocurrencies are being used for financial crimes? And if so, what's being done about it?

Why Cryptocurrency?

Why do white-collar criminals and fraudsters choose to use cryptocurrencies? The media's perception is that currencies like Bitcoin afford criminals a degree of privacy they don't enjoy when using cash or bank transfers.

To an extent, that's true. A bitcoin wallet's ID is a string of characters that on its own is impossible to link to any one person, either a criminal or not. The name that a person uses on an exchange isn't necessarily linkable to a person, either, provided that they don't use something recognisable.

But the anonymity of cryptocurrency is undermined by blockchain. Every transaction is logged and tracked in a publicly accessible, uneditable ledger. As things stand, it is possible to disguise funds and their ultimate destination through a tumbler, but with enough time and effort, any amount of funds can be tracked.

Regardless of how accurate claims of anonymity are, however, those claims are the reason why criminals are attracted to cryptocurrencies. Bitcoin's rise to fame caught the attention of businesses, individuals and fraudsters alike.

Which Financial Crimes?

Cryptocurrencies can be used for almost any type of crime: the most well-known, headline-grabbing crimes are those related to the dark web. Anything to do with hacking and "cyber-crime," terrorism and sexual crime is highlighted extensively.

What isn't highlighted is anything that doesn't grab the imagination. Simple fraud and money laundering don't stir the imagination like those listed above, so even though they're much more common than, say, terrorist funding, they're largely ignored.

In terms of financial crimes, there are several to be aware of, including:

1. Money laundering
2. Bank fraud, i.e. fraudulently accessing and taking the assets of a bank
3. Posing as a bank in order to dupe victims into sending you money (which is also known as "bank fraud")
4. Payment fraud, which is any kind of scam to steal money from a victim, e.g. phishing, ID theft or pagejacking
5. Fraudulent chargebacks, i.e. securing a refund from a business when one isn't necessary, but still keeping the item
6. Funding crimes, e.g. terrorist funding.

Money laundering can be done easily through cryptocurrency. Coins are bought through an exchange and are then put through a tumbler. They are then forwarded in chunks to another wallet not previously used by a known person.

As for terrorist funding, this has been covered extensively in the media. Even though the frequency with which it occurs has likely been overestimated, that doesn't mean it hasn't happened.

Are All Cryptocurrencies Involved in Crime?

All that being said, not all cryptocurrencies are as much involved in financial crime. Bitcoin received a lot of attention for being the first in the market, and for its incredible growth in value. But it's not the most popular with people that want to remain anonymous.

Monero and Z-Cash are currently the most popular privacy-centred cryptoassets available. Each of these privacy-oriented cryptocurrencies has been involved in terrorist funding, specifically ISIS.

It's currently unclear to what extent these currencies are being used for less glamorous, headline-grabbing financial crime. And to be absolutely clear, the people behind these currencies deny that there's a problem. Both are built on blockchain, like all cryptocurrencies.

But any criminal that's knowledgeable about cryptoassets would be attracted to these privacy-centric currencies over others like Bitcoin.

What Is Being Done?

Law enforcement agencies are waking up to the possibilities and dangers of cryptocurrencies. INTERPOL, for example, are actively preparing to meet these dangers. They have set up a special group specifically to look at cryptocurrencies (the *INTERPOL Working Group on Darknet and Cryptocurrencies*).

In 2018 they held a meeting which highlighted Altcoins as a matter of specific concern. But with over 2,000 cryptocurrencies currently available, they have their work cut out identifying which ones are most likely to be used by criminals. In particular, they highlighted Monero and Z-Cash—the two cryptoassets we described above—as worth investigation.

Aside from investigating individual crimes, however, it's unclear how much INTERPOL can do. The task is being left to FinTech, crypto companies and regular financial institutions to identify fraudulent transactions where they can.

Is Extra Government Regulation the Answer?

Some cryptocurrency regulations already exist and lessen the chance of financial crimes.

In the US, for example, Bitcoin exchanges have to be registered with the Financial Crimes Enforcement Network of the US Department of Treasury. But more stringent regulation isn't the answer until tools are available that can pinpoint financial crime and fraud.

With every transaction recorded in the blockchain, though, the capability to do that is there. All we need is the right tools to analyse all the data in front of us. Many IT solutions are currently available in the market, and some of them offer adequate levels of reliability.

You could also argue that government at least needs to make a bigger noise about investigating these claims of white-collar crime. Even if they don't currently have the capability to catch every fraudster, making it obvious that they're trying may at least discourage future criminals.

But as for regulation, there's very little more that governments could do that wouldn't violate the underlying point of cryptocurrencies. The idea is that each coin is independent, devolved, and free of government interference.

It's striking a balance between complete deregulation and the prevention of financial crime that's going to be difficult.

Terrorism and the Dark Web

Nico Prucha

Nico Prucha is a principal at Cognitive Architectures, where he focuses on the linguistic and cultural elements of jihadist activity. He is also a fellow in the department of Near Eastern studies at the University of Vienna in Austria.

G roups such as al-Qaida (AQ) have pursued spectacular attacks to garner media attention and popularize their cause. What is often not noted, however, is that for those who submit themselves to the religious thinking of al-Qaida—and nowadays the self-designated "Islamic State" (IS)—the militant struggle is intertwined with the duty to call upon others to join the movement (da'wa). For jihadists da'wa is obligatory. While AQ's central organization pioneered the use of bulletin forums, blogs, YouTube and to some extent Facebook, for this and other purposes, it was its Syrian branch, Jabhat al-Nusra, that in 2012 pushed effectively into Twitter use. AQ lost its momentum as the social media pioneer of jihadism shortly thereafter to IS. Since 2013, IS has taken the use of social media da'wa and other activities to the next level. From that point onward IS has very effectively projected influence on Twitter on a massive scale, reaching a global audience. Since early 2016, however, IS's networks on Twitter have been degraded by various counter-measures, but the group has reconfigured and shifted to a new social media outlet: Telegram. This application has become the most important information outlet for IS and has been used to recruit and guide attackers in Europe. This article takes a closer look at what Telegram is, and how IS uses it for different purposes: not only operationally, but also for identity building.

"IS and the Jihadist Information Highway—Projecting Influence and Religious Identity via Telegram," by Nico Prucha, Terrorism Research Initiative, June 2016. http://www. terrorismanalysts.com/pt/index.php/pot/article/view/556/html. Licensed under CC BY 3.0 Unported.

"The battle for your reality begins in the fields of digital interaction"

—Douglas Rushkoff "Cyberia"

Introduction

Sunni extremist groups such as al-Qaida (AQ) and the self-proclaimed "Islamic State" (IS) use the Internet as a communication hub to broadcast their messages. Online jihad is a phenomenon that has spread on a massive scale and at fast pace over the past fifteen years. IS in particular puts much effort into its online operation, including maintaining and re-establishing accounts and networks on *Twitter, Facebook, YouTube*, and *Telegram*. Massive amounts of jihadist audio, video and written content can be found on these networks, mostly in Arabic.

IS has moved from *Twitter* to *Telegram*, after a mass amount of account suspensions and more effective spam filters limited the group's appearance on *Twitter*. However, the move to *Telegram* allows IS to operate from the "dark web" and orchestrate media raids and sting attacks into the "surface web," such as *Twitter* and *Facebook*. Several hundred IS channels on Telegram ensure that the content, the videos, and writings of IS are disseminated without much interruption. Among the many messages IS sends, the notion of being a "state" is one of the most appealing ones, as outlined in Jacob Sheikh's contribution in this Special Issue of *Perspectives on Terrorism*.

This content conveys a coherent jihadist worldview, based on theological texts written by AQ ideologues and affiliates as far back as the 1980s. The jihadists' need for spreading theological writings has driven the development of audio-visual productions since the 1980s. A main purpose, back then as well as today, has been identity building: to explain who the "*mujahidin*" are, what they are fighting for, and whom they are fighting against. It is important to stress, that no single political narrative and enemy perception exists among the militants. Rather, groups such as AQ and IS enforce a coherent theology, that constitutes the foundation of what is often referred to as "ideology" in Western discourse, as outlined by Rüdiger Lohlker:

> "Indeed, it is crystal clear—to virtually anyone who has the linguistic capacity to grasp and the opportunity to witness what jihadists are actually saying, writing and doing, both online and offline—that religion matters."

Following 9/11, the Internet became an important platform for AQ to spread its brand of Sunni extremist theology. The online media footprint today is built upon nearly two decades of committed media work by jihadist actors. This dedicated work has been, and is, the expression of a strategic discourse on how to conduct jihadist warfare online, and has been outlined in a highly coherent manner by leading jihadist theoreticians such as Abu Mus'ab al-Suri. This theology, carved out by AQ in the 1980s, entered a new evolutionary phase in 2014 when ISIS declared a "Caliphate." This AQ offshoot then became the central organization's primary rival, developing a massive foothold on social media sites, first Twitter, now Telegram, while AQ has been losing significant support, both online and offline—especially among young extremists. AQ has retained ideological seniority, projected by senior jihadist scholars (*shuyukh al-jihad*), such as Abu Qatada al-Filistini, or Abu Muhammad al-Maqdisi, who criticized IS' declaration of an Islamic state and, for example, lambasted the group for the burning of the captured Jordanian combat pilot in 2015.[8] IS on the other hand has managed to translate territorial control and governance into a coherent, highly professional and structured online output. IS uses AQ's theology for two ends: (i) applied theology: what AQ theorized on paper, IS puts into practice and films it (this is documented by the vast amount of videos released throughout the past three years), and (ii) either re-publishing AQ theological writings (lengthy books, articles, religious guidelines, legal binding documents (*fatwas*), military handbooks etc.), or simply releasing a second, or third edition of an AQ book.

Jihadist videos are a powerful tool—even more so when originating from within territory that is defined as "Islamic." This definition is exemplified in IS videos which, for example, claim to document the application of sharia law, and the enforcement of a life-style in the society under its control that has been romanticized in salafi and salafi-jihadist writings. The massive production and release of videos on *Twitter* in the period 2013-2015 was truly a game changer, as acknowledged by one *Ahrar al-Sham* sympathizer on Twitter:

> "#dangers on the path of jihad; my knowledge on jihad is based on professionally produced jihadist videos affecting the youth more than a thousand books or [religious] sermons."

This led Abu al-Jamajem (Sam Heller, @AbuJamajem) to comment: "Analog jihadists in *Ahrar al-Sham* and *Jabhat al-Nusra* lament ISIS's new, digital world."

Under Abu Bakr al-Baghdadi, IS adopted al-Qaida's iconography and doctrine, without being subject to its formal leadership. The Internet serves as a powerful tool that allows the jihadist network to morph and spread in many directions. IS dedicates time and resources to maintain a persistent output of videos and other items—with *Telegram* being the primary hub to strategically dispatch new content since early 2016.

Strategic Targeting of Selected Audiences Using Foreign Fighters

Cameras are the most effective gateways between real-life and the virtual world. AQ initiated—and theologically sanctioned—using the Internet as a basic tool to call people to come to Islam. This is inseparably tied to militant actions and terrorist operations. IS has learned valuable lessons in using and praising the media work and understands how to use its foreign fighters best: in front of cameras instead of just using them as mere cannon fodder in the front lines. Non-Arab foreign fighters do not, however, appear very often in videos on social media. When they do, they usually convey their individual and personal motivation as to why they have joined IS, explaining in their own words and language to potential recruits in their home countries what "real-Islam" is, while often addressing legitimate and real grievances and injustices endured by Sunni civilians in Syria or other places.

IS has taken the lead in producing mainly Arabic language videos to incite a global Arab audience. IS does so by glamourizing its fighters, ideologues and preachers as ultimate role models, modern-day Islamic warriors, or simply as defenders of Sunni communities in times of suffering. IS presents itself as an Arab movement fighting for independence, yet welcoming non-Arab Muslim foreign fighters into their ranks who are used strategically and on a tactical level for jihadist media, where they can be of value to the state-building efforts. Non-Arab media activists from within the "Caliphate" can call for attacks in their home countries in their respective language or slang and may become guides grooming potential attackers on applications such as *Telegram*.

It must be noted that non-Arab foreign fighters fulfil another role under the guidance of IS media strategists: talking about personal commitment and motivations for having undertaken the emigration (*hijra*) to the "Islamic State" gives such speakers the ability to inspire others to emigrate. Non-Arab foreign fighters tend to be keen to explain in their language aspects of jihadist theology, potentially drawing their audience into reading magazines such as Dabiq to further their education on religious concepts such as "*tawhid*" (monotheism) or "*shirk*" (polytheism).

Influence and Information Campaigns: from Twitter to Telegram

The theology of al-Qaida and subsequently IS, and their ability to propagate that theology as a monopoly of truth through professional promotion and marketing materials disseminated via modern communication technology–has proven to be jihadism's most resilient foundation, and greatest innovation. This jihadist media activism strengthens the movement's resilience on a daily basis with new audio-visual and written propaganda uploaded from a number of conflict zones, in numerous languages, to a wide range of online social platforms and multimedia channels.

In the West, policy makers are struggling to cope with the massive quantity and often times high quality productions issued by groups such IS who continue to draw in new recruits from Western societies, especially from Europe. Policy-makers have slowly recognized that the so-called "counter narratives" are failing, as highlighter by *New York Times* in 2015. IS has proven its resilience on the battlefield and the West has so far employed half-hearted "counter-narratives," that usually neither touch upon the Arabic propaganda content, nor the messages conveyed by non-Arab foreign fighters, who explain their reasons for joining the cause in their own words. Due to the tactical focus of both "counter-narratives" and takedowns of IS messages from the Internet, the US and its Western allies are being drawn into open online warfare, on a battlefield chosen by their jihadist adversaries. Those jihadists who will probably thrive in the resulting chaos. The ideology/theology of IS, offering a coherent worldview, while IS had been gaining and consolidating territory, has proven time and again to be resilient on all layers on the Internet.

From 2011 onwards, the main platform for Sunni jihadists online was *Twitter*, in addition to *Facebook* and *YouTube*, especially since the outbreak of violence in Syria. This propagation effort by the so-called "*media mujahidin*" has been approved and sanctioned by the movement's leaders, and now feeds an interconnected jihadist Zeitgeist. For example, jihadist groups had been using *Twitter* to disseminate links to video content shot on the battlefield in Syria and posted such video footage for mass consumption on *YouTube*. Since 2011, members of jihadist forums have issued media strategy advice that encourages the development of *media mujahidin*. This has been accompanied by the release of guides on how to use social media platforms, which often included lists of recommended accounts to follow. With relatively small efforts, IS was able to maintain massive networks on *Twitter*. This gave the media operations a whole new and unprecedented window of opportunity: the releasing of videos from within what is defined as "Islamic territory," liberated from their enemies, to a massive number of active or passive followers.

Twitter did, after a while, an excellent job in preventing IS from keeping up its extensive networks on the service, despite the commitment and dedication of some of the media mujahidin to re-open hundreds of new accounts. This too changed when *Twitter* became more effective at banning IS content by adjusting its spam settings, severely weakening the jihadists' network on the platform. The degrading of IS *Twitter* networks led many Western observers on Twitter to believe IS in general was in decline. However, while the '*Twitter*ship' was sinking for IS, the jihadi online swarm simply turned to a new social media platform—*Telegram*.

In early 2016 a massive shift from *Twitter* to *Telegram* among IS militants and sympathizers could be observed. Until then IS had been able to maintain a persistent network on *Twitter*, despite a steadily growing rate of account suspensions. Because *media mujahidin* are highly dedicated—as much as *mujahidin* are on the battlefield—IS *Twitter* users usually reappeared on the platform, using a different account once their original account had been banned. From a user perspective, all you needed to be aware of was a good set of Arabic and non-Arabic key words to find IS content on *Twitter*, and then start following the accounts. At the same time, the IS network on *Twitter* was not taken down at once, and the remaining accounts keenly promoted the new Twitter handles of those who returned.

Substituting the Jihadist Twittersphere for Islamic State Telegrams

Telegram offers privacy and encryption, allowing users to interact, using their mobile devices (tablets and smartphones) as well as laptop and desktop computers. It offers a secure environment where sharing content is very easy. This includes the option to download large files directly via the *Telegram* application instead of having to open an external link in a browser to access the new videos and word documents. According to *Telegram*, the application is a cloud-based instant messaging service, providing optional end-to-end-encrypted messaging. It is free and open, having an "open API and protocol free for everyone," while having no limits on how much data individual users can share.

Media savvy IS members and sympathizers then took to *Telegram* where in the meantime, via hundreds of channels, often more than 30,000 *Telegram* messages are being pushed out by them each week. *Telegram* is being used to share content produced by "official" IS channels. As had been the case on *Twitter*—and as is the nature of online jihad on social media sites—such content is enriched and enhanced by media supporters from within ISIS held territory, as well as by sympathisers worldwide. The output is mainly in Arabic whereas dedicated linguist and translation departments ensure that a global audience is reached. *Telegram* is being used as a formal communication channel by a range of content aggregators within the movement, rolling out the official IS videos from the various provinces to Microsoft Word and PDF documents released by a rich blend of media agencies, such as al-*Battar, al-Wafa', Ashhad, al-Hayyat* and many more.

A media group by the name *Horizon (Mu'assassat Afaaq)* established itself as a new IS media wing to provide sympathisers with advice and tutorials on online security and encryption. This is a current trend and highlights that user security on mobile devices, encryption and general awareness is rising. Arguably, this chatter on *Telegram* also led "classic" IS media newspapers to pick up this trend and their messaging put more emphasis on the "electronic war," enemy capabilities and operational security, accompanied by relevant advice for IS members and sympathizers.

Arabic transcribed keywords in Latin such as "*ghazwa*" play a major role, and help identify content quickly and sign up for new jihadist related channels on *Telegram*. As visualized above—taken from the IS channel *Ghazwa* on Telegram, the transliteration can vary especially after channels are being suspended, yet the words are easily identified by Arabic-speakers.

The "*Ghazwa*" channel on *Telegram* alludes to the classical understanding of conducting raids in the desert. It celebrates the early Muslims raiders, being *murabitin*, horsemen ready for war while spiritually tuned to defend territory and willing to enter Paradise.

Jihadists perceive *Telegram* as a coordination point for raids (*ghazawat*), enabling the injection of content in an orchestrated manner onto social media platforms. *Telegram* is central to the supply of text for *Tweets*, disseminating new hashtags, the timing of such raids, and the flooding of comments on *Facebook* pages and so on. However, IS media operatives and sympathizers miss *Twitter*. IS official media outlets has called for a return to *Twitter*—fearing that da'wa on *Telegram* just reaching like-minded sympathizers will not work (more on this below).

During the attacks in March 2016 in Brussels, IS media operatives on *Telegram* prepared French language Tweets with hashtags used at the time of the attack to maximize the reach of pro-IS Tweets. Likewise, other social media platforms are affected by such "social media raids." By the time accounts were deleted on *Twitter* and elsewhere, IS had a new event-driven operation backed by social media raids. While the attacks in Paris and Brussels were major external events, most IS-driven and mediatized events are occurring in the Arab countries. A day before the November 2015 Paris attack, IS had dispatched suicide bombers to strike in Beirut, followed by social media raids. Since the beginning of the Iraqi Army operations to reclaim Mosul from IS on October 16, 2016, most event driven media raids are related thereto. As had been the case on *Twitter, Telegram* is now the main hub for IS to share content reposting from *Twitter*, other social media such as *YouTube, Vimeo, DailyMotion, SendVid* and *Facebook*, as well as websites containing IS propaganda, including those hosted on *WordPress.com*.

The multi-lingual strategic outreach and communication approach has a clear objective: targeting non-Arabic speaking potential recruits in the West. This remains a high priority for IS, while also maintaining and ensuring the steady and uninterrupted production and dissemination of Arabic content (targeting Arab native speakers worldwide).

How Does IS Use the Platform to Recruit European Foreign Fighters and Terrorists?

Throughout the Summer of 2016, alleged "lone wolf" attackers struck in France, Germany, Russia and the US. The attackers acted on behalf of IS and in most cases selfie-styled videos had been made and uploaded by them to IS media operatives of *Amaq Agency (wakalat al-ʿAmaq)*. The short videos followed a classical Jihadist template, with the variation that these had not been foreign fighters, but rather local French, American, Chechen citizens, or as in the case of Germany, refugees from Syria or Afghanistan.

Omar Mateen, US citizen born in America, attacked a night club in Orland, Florida in June 2016, leaving 49 people dead and 53 injured. Jihadist users on *Telegram* were quick to disseminate pictures of Omar Mateen—after these had been released by the mainstream media—to praise the attacker as a martyr and "soldier of the Caliphate." A trend on *Telegram* quickly emerged to refer to such attacks under the hashtag "in your homes," a reference to the jihadist division of world into "*dar al-Islam*" (abode of Islam) and "*dar al-kuffar*" (abode of disbelievers).

As French, American and other anti-IS coalition combat aircraft continue to bomb the "*dar al-Islam*," IS seeks to inspire and theologically guide supporters such as Omar Mateen to conduct revenge operations in the "depth of your abodes" (*fi ʿaqr diyarikum*), as the Arabic hashtag for "in your homes" advocates. Whatever the jihadists produce for publication, it always must be theologically coherent. The concept of *dar* (abode) is an identity marker for the Islamic State.

According to IS, "Islam" has been restored and is now embodied by its "state." IS presents itself as the only legitimate zone where Sunni Muslims can exercise their duties towards God since

> "….the whole world, from east to west, became dar al-kufr, the "abode of the disbelievers." Therefore God set in motion the establishment of the Islamic State. This state consists of numerous elements that make it dar al-Islam."

The Syrian refugee who failed undertaking a suicide bombing attack in Ansbach, Germany, as well as the Afghan refugee who at random stabbed passengers on train in the region of Würzburg had filmed their final statements beforehand. These statements are—just like the 9/11 "martyr's" videotaped farewell message or the 7/7/ bombing attackers last words—testimony (*wasiyya*) as much as legacy. Clearly IS pursues a strategy of seeking to recruit refugees, or dispatching sleeper cells posing as refugees coming to Europe, knowing this results in an increase of polarization within Western societies.

Allegedly, *Telegram* was used to communicate from within the "Caliphate" with at least some of the attackers, who then in turn used the app to upload their self-filmed *wasiyya*. This video was then edited and branded with the *Amaq* logo and released to the IS *Telegram* community with the intention that the swarm would fan it out to other online sites and platforms for maximum visibility.

The value of continuing its successful influence operation has driven IS on *Telegram* to dedicate media channels and media operatives to translating and producing new content for specific French, German, Italian, English, Russian, and Bahasa Indonesian audiences.

This has led to a two-tier production line: (i) official and (ii) user generated content. Together, these packages carry a range of messages which focus on the importance of the individual to initiate action. They echo the ethos captured in the "Open Source Jihad" as set by AQ's English language magazine *Inspire*, where barriers to entry are low and anyone can contribute. For example, they encourage individuals to realise that not all attacks have to be complex coordinated operations, nor use sophisticated weaponry, nor focus on a specific high profile target. Instead they articulate that anyone can strike a blow for IS.

On November 26, 2016, IS released a video in French with Arabic subtitles. The video was published *Furat Media*—a dedicated IS-media institution that produces content for non-Arab(ic) audience. As usual, the video is in 16:9 format, full high definition, and features praise for the spate of "lone wolf" attackers in 2016. The film, entitled "Sur leur pas" and على خطاهم in Arabic, demonstrates vividly how IS uses *Telegram* to instigate attacks.

Assailants are introduced and areas of attacks highlighted. Combined with mainstream media footage of completed attacks, IS portrays these as revenge operations and part of the Islamic State's "foreign policy." *Telegram* chat exchanges claim to "document" that some aspiring IS fighters had expressed the wish to conduct the *hijra* (emigration) and join IS, but had been warned this was too dangerous. Instead, they may have been swayed to launch attacks in their home countries rather than risking arrest while seeking to emigrate. The video concludes with a young man watching an IS video on his laptop. His gun rests besides his laptop, suggesting he is ready to stage an attack as revenge for the many atrocities against Sunni Muslims, he has just been lectured about via the laptop.

[...]

Conclusion

Unlike AQ, IS controls swathes of territory in the Sunni Arab heartlands, primarily in Iraq and Syria. The theology which was largely theoretical in the case of AQ is now applied in full by IS—making the "state" a real and, to IS-sympathizers, attractive alternative where the imaginary "real-Islam" promoted by AQ has now become a reality with IS. Sunni extremism is driven by an absolute belief in God for which the application of absolute formalized religious rule is the desired final objective (and the only solution to minimize the risk of living in a state of sin, which would mean ending up in hellfire). For more than three decades, jihadists, in their own words, both in their writings and in their video productions, have been yearning for the creation of an Islamic State and, ultimately, the return of the Caliphate. The self-designated "Islamic State" claims to answer to this desire for the restoration of Islam to a position of power.

The existence of a coherent set of powerful jihadist narratives, combined with the unprecedented achievement of the Islamic State to ensure a persistent presence on social media and the Internet in general, make the task of effectively countering IS a big challenge. Any approach taken needs to combine hard and soft measures (counter-terrorism and counter-narratives). Improving nascent efforts at producing counter-narratives can be one step in the right direction in the soft-power domain. These efforts need to engage in religious discourses, as religion is one of the central elements in IS' efforts to recruit and radicalize its potential followers. Unless the religious dimension is properly acknowledged and addressed, the legacy of IS will not die with the fall of the territorial Caliphate that is now under attack from coalition forces. As also highlighted in Jakob Sheikh's contribution to this Special Issue of *Perspectives on Terrorism*, the idea of an Islamic State, is rooted in a broad Sunni jihadist tradition that has been gaining strength for more than 35 years and has become a major pull-factor for militant recruitment.

Neglecting the fact that jihadist online networks are forming a whole as they are basing themselves on a coherent theological framework will allow IS to survive a recover even after territorial extinction. In the words of Rüdiger Lohlker: "Without deconstructing the theology of violence inherent in jihadi communications and practice, these religious ideas will continue to inspire others to act, long after any given organized force, such as the Islamic State, may be destroyed on the ground."

Law Enforcement Activity on the Dark Web Raises Ethical Questions

Kat Hadjimatheou

Dr. Kat Hadjimatheou is a research fellow with the Interdisciplinary Ethics Research Group at the University of Warwick in the UK. Her work focuses on the ethics of policing, security technologies, border control, trafficking, and surveillance. In addition to her academic work, she has consulted on a number of European Union–funded security projects.

[...]

The Dark Web refers to a layer of the Internet in which content has been intentionally concealed and users can surf anonymously. In order to reach the DW and to access its content, one needs to install a certain program whose function is similar to that of a web browser or search engine. The most commonly known program is The Onion Browser (TOR) (MEDI@4SEC D1.1). The feature that distinguishes the Dark Web from the open web is therefore encryption. While there is nothing ethically or legally dubious about encryption in principle, the reality is that much of the activity on the Dark Web by people in liberal democracies is unethical and/or illegal.

The Dark Web hosts a vast range of sites and forums for unethical and illegal behaviour, from illicit markets for drugs, counterfeit goods, and contract killings to money laundering, extremist sites and forums for the sharing of child sexual abuse material. All of these activities are legitimate targets of policing, and all are made easier to perform and more difficult to prevent and prosecute by encryption. However, it is not only criminals who use the dark net. Political dissidents and activists, journalists, law

"Policing the Dark Web: Ethical and Legal Issues," by Kat Hadjimatheou, MEDI@4SEC. Reprinted by permission.

enforcement and the military also take advantage of the security and anonymity offered by encryption.

[…]

Ethical and Legal Issues with LEA Operations on the Dark Web

[…]

Distinction Between Ethics and Law

The ethical and legal issues discussed here are distinct but related. Ethics relates to the reasons we have for thinking something is the right or wrong thing to do. Law relates to the rules a society has in place with which people can be coerced legitimately by the state into complying. Some ethical issues are reflected in the law; but ethics is broader than law: while illegal behaviour is typically also unethical, much unethical behaviour is not regulated by the law. For example, ethics tells us that breaking a promise is nearly always wrongful, even if it is sometimes justified overall given the costs of keeping the promise in the particular circumstances. Thus, ethical considerations *always* come into play when promise-making and promise-breaking are concerned. In contrast, legal considerations only arise when the promises in question fall within the narrower set that are legally enforceable, say in the form of contracts. Ethics is thus broader than the law, providing perspectives from which to criticize the law and argue for its reform.

To say that something is legally permissible is to say that it can be done without legal consequence. Thus legal analysis can tell us what the law requires and so what we need to do if we want to avoid being prosecuted, sued, and so on. Ethics cannot do this. But because the law usually reflects some minimum threshold of acceptability, the fact that something is lawful does not by itself demonstrate that it is desirable- let alone morally laudable or an example of best practice. Ethics can offer guidance as to what we are permitted to do, encouraged to do and required to do, morally speaking. Thus it can offer advice about what kinds of things public security providers and technology developers should do if they want their actions to be both legal and examples of best practice. Many police codes of ethics and codes of conduct include both minimum standards of behaviour and more aspirational principles. In practice, there is significant crossover between ethics and the law. For example, Privacy by Design (an approach to projects, including technology design, that promotes privacy and data protection compliance from the start) is an approach that began as best practice but is now being incorporated into EU Data Protection law.[1] And ethics can have a key role to play in informing the law when, as is so often the case, the latter lags behind technological development.

A crossover between ethics and law also arises when both sets of principles, rules or norms share common roots. The legal issues raised in this report are grounded in and make reference to international, EU, and domestic legal instruments. The ethical issues are grounded in the values of liberal democratic political theory, including in particular equal treatment, fairness, autonomy and liberty.[2] Because the legal instruments referred to in this report are those of progressive liberal democracies, the legal and ethical concerns described below are closely related and sometimes overlap.

Sometimes the values underpinning ethics and the law conflict, and ethical and legal debates are often concerned with finding the best way to reconcile conflicting duties and obligations. Within liberal democratic societies the question of which rights, rules and requirements these values give rise to is also often subject to debate. Finally, the interpretation of the role and status of the police and the nature and source of their authority varies significantly between liberal democratic countries. As this suggests, shared roots and basic commitments do not preclude dilemmas and disagreements within both ethics and the law.

[…]

Harms Arising from Use of Unusual and/ or Unorthodox Disruption Techniques

Certain features of the Dark Web, in particular the difficulty of tracing activities back to identifiable people and locations, and the internationally distributed nature of criminal activity, make it difficult to apply traditional LEA approaches. As a result, activities designed to disrupt illicit activity by taking advantage of anonymity and the fragile basis of trust on the Dark Web have become more attractive to LEAs. These might include:

- spreading misinformation, fake news, and rumour to fuel mistaken beliefs about police activities online and to reduce trust between e.g. buyers and sellers of illicit products.
- using technological means, such as DDS techniques which overwhelm outlets and force them to close, in order to disrupt the supply chain online.
- using "honey pot" techniques, such as using automatic tools to pretend to be vendors and "sell" drugs, so that users get scammed and don't return to the market.
- advertising LEA's own successes to show that they operate confidently on the Dark Web, which would reduce trust in encryption. For example, the Dutch national police have created a dark web site that lists Dark Web vendors by pseudonym, including those under investigation, those who are "identified," and 15 who have already been arrested in current and past investigations. "We trace people who are active at Dark Markets and offer illicit goods or services," the site reads. "Are you one of them? Then you have our attention."[3]

Such tactics might be effective in deterring crime on the Dark Web, however they may also have negative implications, which are now considered below.

The Risk of Criminalizing Innocuous Behaviour and/or Undermining the Exercise of Valuable Freedoms Facilitated by the Dark Web

Not all activity on the Dark Web is suspect. Some citizens use the Dark Web as they do the open web. For example, ethnographic research on one particular Dark Web site—the Dark Web Social Network—in 2014, describes a politically libertarian but innocuous website, used by people who see it as a means of being free from the kind of corporate and government surveillance they find objectionable on the open web. As that research reports, the Dark Web Social Network's "about" page describes it as "a safe and moderated environment for the productive exchange of information."[4] Notably, that research also found that the Dark Web Social Network discouraged child sexual exploitation images and policed itself relatively successfully. Similar processes of moral policing on the Dark Web were also reported in more recent research based on interviews with administrators of Dark Web search engines.[5] And tech commentators and researchers routinely predict that more and more everyday and innocuous "surface web" activity will migrate to the Dark Web as people become more concerned about their privacy and less tolerant of corporate monitoring of their behaviour for marketing purposes.[6] Privacy and censorship concerns also are emerging as significant predictors of reduced opposition to the Dark Web[7], as a reported surge of Dark Web usage following the Edward Snowden revelations appears to confirm.[8]

For many using the Dark Web, their activities are not only innocuous but also constitute the exercise of valuable freedoms. Chief amongst these are the freedom to express political views or sexual preferences without fear of persecution by authoritarian regimes and the freedom to exchange information without manipulation or monitoring by profit-seeking companies. Some Dark Web users consider the term "dark net" or "Dark Web" itself a media fabrication to draw attention away from the legitimate, innocuous, and even life-saving use of the Dark

Web and towards the criminal. Some, like Edward Snowden and Julian Assange, see government-sponsored attempts to crack anonymity on the Dark Web as an attack on freedoms, especially privacy.[9]

An LEA approach to the Dark Web that treated all activity there as suspect in an undifferentiated, blanket manner would risk undermining the exercise of these freedoms. For example, attempting to crack encryption and expose the identities of individuals interacting anonymously on the Dark Web might not only expose those particular individuals to harms from authoritarian governments, but also undermine the trust that is vital to the effective function of the Dark Web as a space safe from political persecution. For this reason, LEAs in liberal democratic jurisdictions should as far as possible adopt a targeted approach to policing the Dark Web, focusing on exposing, disrupting and prosecuting criminals while refraining from interfering with innocuous activities and the exercise of political freedoms.

[…]

Notes

1. See http://ec.europa.eu/justice/data-protection/reform/index_en.htm.

2. Seminal philosophers in this field include: John Locke; Immanuel Kant; John Rawls; Ronald Dworkin; J.S. Mill.

3. Greenberg in Wired Magazine, 2017, https://www.wired.com/story/alphabay-hansa-takedown-darkweb-trap/.

4. Gehl, Robert. (2016a) "Power/freedom on the dark web: A digital ethnography of the Dark Web Social Network." New Media & Society, 18(7).

5. Gehl, Robert, (2016) "Is the Dark Web legit? The case of Dark Web search engines." Selected Papers of AoIR 2016: The 17th Annual Conference of the Association of Internet Researchers Berlin, Germany / 5-8 October 2016.

6. Bartlett, Jamie, "How the mysterious dark bet is going mainstream," TED talk, available at: https://www.ted.com/talks/jamie_bartlett_how_the_mysterious_dark_net_is_going_mainstream.

7. Jardine Eric. (2017) "Privacy, censorship, data breaches and Internet freedom: The drivers of support and opposition to Dark Web technologies." *New Media and Society*. Online First. October 4, 2017.

8. Gehl, 2016a (as above).

9. http://www.rollingstone.com/politics/news/the-battle-for-the-dark-net-20151022. Retrieved 11-10- 2016.

The Value of the Dark Web

Andrew Murray

Andrew Murray is professor of law and media technology at the London School of Economics and specialist advisor to the House of Lords Communication Inquiry "Regulating in a Digital World."

On Wednesday the Prime Minister announced that a new police and intelligence unit formed by GCHQ and the National Crime Agency would be set up to police the Dark Net. It is needed, according to the Prime Minister, because the Dark Net is full of "sickening" images that are shared by paedophiles. To quote from his speech: "The dark net is the next side of the problem, where paedophiles and perverts are sharing images, not using the normal parts of the internet that we all use." This is clearly a tightly co-ordinated government policy move designed to tie in with the WeProtect Summit, which saw delegates from law enforcement and technology companies from more than fifty countries descend on Whitehall. The question, though, is this a policy development we demand or even need?

The dark net is an area often misunderstood by government and by the public at large. Headlines tend to be lurid "Unravelling the Dark Web: Forget South American cartels and Russian arms dealers: the black market has moved online" or "The disturbing world of the Deep Web, where contract killers and drug dealers ply their trade on the internet." In truth the reality of the dark net is rather more prosaic.

There is, as with all areas of life, a criminal element within the dark web. Probably though no more than there is in the surface web. Yes you can find sites offering drugs or images of child abuse but you can also find these things on the surface web. The dark web, which is accessed though anonymisation software such as

"The Dark Web Is Not Just for Paedophiles, Drug Dealers and Terrorists," by Andrew Murray, *The Independent*, December 12, 2014. Reprinted by permission.

Tor, also offers essential privacy and anonymity to persons at risk and to ordinary people like you and me.

Reporters Without Borders recommend the use of Tor as part of its "survival kit" for bloggers, journalists and activists in countries where they may be at risk from state censorship or even arrest. The International Broadcasting Bureau (who broadcast Voice of America and Radio Free Asia) is a major Tor sponsor and recommends its use by persons in repressive regimes to allow them access to global media. Tor is also recommended by Human Rights Watch and by Global Voices.

It is not only human rights organisations and media groups who recommend its use; IT professionals and business executives also use Tor to, among other things, test firewalls, provide emergency internet access during DNS failures and provide confidentiality.

The clearest picture of the value of the anonymised deep web, or dark web if you must, is to be found in the Tor Project's financial reports. Here we see that the project received over $1.8m from the US Government in 2013, equating to over 50 per cent of total income. The grants come from a number of resources including over $555,000 from Internetwork News, a non-profit democracy and human rights group funded by the US State Department and over $830,000 from SRI international, which is funded by the US Department of Defense.

If you think it seems quite unlikely that the US Government would be funding a service which supports paedophiles, drug dealers and terrorists, that's because—as I hope you're beginning to see—that's not what the dark net is.

Reporting that part of the dark net without context is like reporting only the criminal activity that happens in a town or city without also reporting on the vibrant community, culture and commerce that thrives there. As with all communities there is a criminal element, but the dark net community is much more.

The problem is unlike a real world town or city most people either can't or don't want to visit the dark net so their perception is driven by one-sided reporting. We imagine the worst and fail to see the best. It is this perception that is driving the policy shift signalled in the last 48 hours. The Prime Minister and Home Secretary are signalling an attack on the soft underbelly of the dark net. No one is going to stand up and defend the actions of paedophiles, so announcing a policy designed to attack paedophiles and to remove child abuse images is going to get little to no negative reaction.

However two things must be borne in mind. The first is that in 2004 BT introduced its Anti-Child Abuse Initiative, colloquially known as Cleanfeed, to block access to child abuse images held on surface web servers overseas. This was met with almost universal acclaim but in 2008 this system prevented UK Wikipedia users from editing pages on the site for nearly four days. Although arguably a correct application of the principles the system was designed for, it had clearly over-regulated. Moreover the changes in the application of Cleanfeed from 2011 onwards, in particular its use to block file sharing websites, is a clear development of a technology designed for a laudable purpose; to police paedophiles, to another less clear-cut application the policing of file sharing.

The second is the particular announcement of the Prime Minister that GCHQ will form part of the new deep web policing unit. Post the Edward Snowden revelations the use of anonymisation tools such as Tor rose substantially with some reports suggesting they have increased by 100 per cent or more. Documents released by Snowden and reported in the Guardian suggested that the NSA were targeting Tor before this.

A cynical observer may suggest that a non-controversial, even welcome, plan to track paedophiles in the dark web may provide GCHQ with the Trojan horse they need to infiltrate and eventually strip away the anonymity that Tor offers to journalists, bloggers, activists and privacy advocates. If this happens the dark web may no longer be dark but it may also no longer be safe.

Law Enforcement Must Respect the Privacy Rights of Dark Web Users

Michael Chertoff

Michael Chertoff is a former US circuit judge who also served as US secretary of Homeland Security under President George W. Bush. He is one of the authors of the USA Patriot Act and cofounder of the Chertoff Group, a risk management and security consulting firm.

[…]

Policy Issues Pertaining to the Dark Web

Creating policy to address the Dark Web requires an understanding of the benefits and risks of anonymity and of an open internet. Rash and sweeping legislation has the potential to encroach on civil liberties and to be a nightmare to enforce. On the other hand, not addressing the Dark Web will allow illicit activities to persist unabated. It is impossible to regulate the Dark Web in isolation; any regulations must be applicable to the internet as a whole and will thus affect Surface Web users, Deep Web researchers, and Dark Web criminals alike. This section will explore two important policy issues surrounding the Dark Web: the appropriate role of government, and the tactics that government enforcers should employ.

Major Policy Issues 1: What Is the Appropriate Role for the Government in the Dark Web?

When new technologies arise, the government must determine its role in regulating them. Technological progress can change the ways our laws apply and necessitate new laws. For example, the United States is still struggling to adapt old laws governing telephones and television to the internet. The Dark Web is a brand new topic to many policy-makers, and it is essential that they

"A Public Policy Perspective of the Dark Web," by Michael Chertoff, *Journal of Cyber Policy*, Taylor & Francis, March 13, 2017. Reprinted by permission.

become informed before enacting policy rather than learning from mistakes. Current US laws are vaguely applicable to the Dark Web, but government agencies have not solidified policies on how to regulate it within a legal framework.

The most important Dark Web policy issue is regulating Tor. The Dark Web could not exist without anonymising technology. Anonymity is the crux of what makes the Dark Web different from the Surface Web, so policy regarding anonymity and, by extension, the use of Tor, is most relevant. There are two central challenges to creating policy for the Dark Web: protecting anonymity and working internationally. Policies regarding the Dark Web must be clear and internationally agreeable, without compromising the ideals of the American people.

The first challenge is that there is nothing inherently criminal about using Tor for anonymity, but there is no clear way to sort the criminals from the innocent users if they are all anonymous. If there were no criminals using Tor, the law enforcement community would not be pushing so hard against the anonymity that it provides. Unfortunately, it is very difficult to hold someone accountable for their actions if their identity is unknown, and it is hard to unmask one person without having the capability to deanonymise everyone else using Tor.

The second challenge is that the internet is inherently very international, which makes coordinating regulations challenging. One country does not control the entire internet, and as much as some nations would like to have full control over the ideas coming in and out of their country, they have not fully achieved success with a "great firewall." The internet cannot be regulated country by country without destroying the benefits that the internet brings to all countries, so finding consensus is important. There is some content, such as images of child abuse, that all countries agree should be illegal and banned across all distribution outlets. There is other content however, like political dissidence, where different countries have dramatically different stances.

The United States currently has some laws that are applicable to Dark Web activity, but they were not specifically designed to meet the challenge of the Dark Web. For example, hacking is often enabled by the Dark Web. Hackers will purchase malware from other hackers, or will use a Dark Web method of collecting ransom from ransomware attacks. Hacking is regulated by the Computer Fraud and Abuse Act (CFAA), which bans trespassing on, unauthorised accessing of, and damaging computers in interstate or international commerce. The CFAA also bars trafficking, unauthorised computer access, and computer espionage. These US regulations are perfectly sufficient to handle hacking, but they do not specifically tackle the challenge of anonymity online, and they are not necessarily effective beyond US borders, from where most cybercrime against the US is launched. Regulating cybercrime on the Dark Web therefore becomes exponentially more challenging when the international community is brought in.

[…]

The United States must rise to the challenge of enacting policy that successfully strikes the balance between protecting user anonymity and preventing illegal activity online. Nations around the globe have different stances on how best to tackle the challenge of Tor. Given that international cooperation will be essential, governments must work together towards creating smart Dark Web policy. The specific tactics for intervening on the Dark Web must be carefully considered. Many governments, including the U.S. government, have made attempts in the past with varying degrees of success. By learning from past mistakes, leaders can create policy that effectively addresses the challenge of tomorrow's internet.

Major Policy Issue 2: What Are the Appropriate Tactics for Government Intervention on the Dark Web?

Once the United States government has determined its role in regulating the Dark Web, it must decide which tactics it will use to carry out that role. The government must use tactics that take down criminal Dark Web activity while protecting the anonymity of innocent users to the maximum extent possible. In the interest of not compromising any confidential information, the tactics explored in this section are those that have been publicly released. This section will discuss the lessons that can be learned from previously used tactics. The most effective and reasonable tactics are those that can target specific anonymous users and hold them accountable for their actions rather than deanonymising vast swathes of user data.

The combined capabilities of a small handful of government agencies can be effectively employed towards the end of policing the Dark Web. The FBI has had the capability to use a computer and internet protocol address verifier (CIPAV) to "identify suspects who are disguising their location using proxy servers or anonymity services, like Tor" since 2002. This technology allows Tor traffic to be flagged separately from regular internet traffic. It does nothing to compromise the anonymity of users, but it is helpful in narrowing down search parameters when the FBI performs an investigation. The Department of Defense's Defense Advanced Research Projects Agency (DARPA) is developing a tool called Memex, which can uncover patterns to help law enforcement combat illegal activity. This project is another way that investigative agencies could make sense of Tor traffic without having to unmask all Tor users. Instead, investigators could detect specific patterns and then track down the specific user making the suspicious requests.

An important case study occurred in February of 2015. The FBI used a hacking tool to identify the IP addresses of users accessing a hidden Tor child abuse site called Playpen. Within a month of being launched in 2014, Playpen had 60,000 member accounts. By 2015, there were 215,000 accounts, 117,000 posts, and 11,000 unique visitors per week. In order to take down the site, the FBI took the unprecedented move of seizing the Playpen server and transferring the site to an FBI server, under a warrant issued by a federal magistrate judge in the Eastern District of Virginia. The FBI ran Playpen off their server from 20th February to 4th

March of 2015 and were able to access the computers of about 1000 Playpen users during that time. That resulted in sufficient evidence to bring about 1500 cases against people accessing images of child abuse on Playpen. This tactic managed to capture only those who were accessing the child abuse site while leaving other users of Tor untouched. While some may have ethical qualms about the FBI running a child abuse server for a couple weeks, there is a strong argument to be made that by identifying the users, the FBI was able to prevent further access to images of child abuse in the future. As a result, Tor users will feel slightly less protected by their anonymity when they are accessing illegal sites, but other people who browse using Tor regularly can still enjoy comfort and anonymity in their legal activities.

Legal frameworks are essential in supporting criminal investigations. There is a debate over whether the federal magistrate judge from the Eastern District of Virginia had the legal authority to issue a warrant that led to searches outside the judge's district. This is an example of current US laws not keeping up with evolving technology. The FBI maintains that the warrant was valid because the server was being run from a site located in the judge's district. However, in the nine cases that have been brought so far using evidence from this sting operation, six judges have written opinions to indicate that the first federal judge did not have the authority to authorise searches outside his jurisdiction. The problem that arises from this debate is that it would have been impossible to identify the users of Playpen, and then get warrants for each user, if it had not been for the tool that the FBI installed on the server. To be clear, the FBI later got individual warrants to search the computer of every suspect identified in the case. A policy solution must be found which gives the FBI a stronger legal footing for employing such an effective investigative technique in the future.

The takedown of Silk Road was a case where FBI tactics were somewhat less than fully successful. To be sure, the operator, Ross Ulbricht, was arrested, but since the FBI shut down Silk Road in October of 2013, there has been an explosion in the darknet market for illegal goods. The market was previously centralised around Silk Road, but it has become more fragmented. There is a Reddit directory of Dark Web marketplaces that is updated to inform users which ones are reputable and which ones are unreliable, and the list of untrusted sites is far longer than the list of trusted ones. Almost immediately after Silk Road was shut down, users flocked to a previously unknown site called the Sheep Marketplace. This site dominated the Dark Web market until a vendor exploited a vulnerability and stole $6 million in bitcoins. Silk Road 2.0 was launched by former administrators of the original Silk Road on 6th November 2013. This came only one month after the original Silk Road was shut down. Silk Road 2.0 was short-lived. It was hacked in February 2014 by a vendor who stole $2.7 million in users' bitcoins. That was not the end of the Silk Road however. Silk Road 3.0 is considered the most resilient Dark Net market and has been operational since May 2016.Thus, while the government took down the original Silk Road, it is clear that that operation was not entirely successful, as it did little to dissuade people from starting new Dark Web marketplaces, and it did not hold vendors or customers accountable for their transactions on the site. As Eric Jardine points out, these criminal activities conducted on the Dark Web may be knocked down, but other programmes emerge and simply take their place.

Another unsuccessful case of government intervention in Dark Web matters came in March of 2015 when federal investigators served a subpoena to Reddit in which they demanded the personal data of five users who accessed r/darknetmarkets, a forum where users discussed illegal online marketplaces. This was an unwise action because it discourages future discussion on open forums such as Reddit. If criminals are driven away from open and easy-to-monitor pages and towards pages that are hidden in the Dark Web, it makes the FBI's job of finding cybercriminals much more challenging.

The three case studies described above cover the spectrum from effective to ineffective enforcement. The best tactics are those that are narrowly focused, like the ones the FBI employed to take down Playpen. In other words, these tactics search for the criminals in places where anyone visiting the site is a criminal. This is the best of both worlds because it allows for long-term deterrence while protecting user privacy to the maximum extent reasonable. In the interest of continuing to be effective, the FBI must be given a stronger legal framework to perform such investigations. The tactic that was used with Silk Road, of merely taking down a site, has a short-term pay-off, but it is largely ineffective in the long run because other marketplaces will pop up to meet the demand. The tactic that was employed with the Reddit forum was essentially a failure. It did nothing to deter illegal activity, and it squandered an opportunity to monitor discussion in the open and more tactfully identify those involved with illegal activity. In examining these cases, it is clear that tactful, carefully directed operations will be most successful in deterring future illegal activity on the Dark Web while being mindful of innocent users' privacy.

Conclusion

The Dark Web is, by its nature, anonymous and incapable of discriminating between criminals and ordinary users. Enforcement agencies must address this issue by employing tactics that maintain the privacy of the average user while unmasking the criminal.

The most effective way of doing this is by looking for the illegal sites instead of the illegal users. Under proper legal authority, government hackers can place deanonymising tools onto the computers of users accessing the site. If the government merely shuts down the site, another will pop up in its place. On the other hand, if enforcers bring charges against the users of an illicit site, future users who are considering accessing illegal sites will be more hesitant to do so because of the risk of getting caught. The final option would be for the government to attempt to break Tor, in other words, to identify every Tor user. This, given the past trend with Silk Road, would likely result in a more robust version of the service being created, thwarting the government's efforts. It would also destroy a useful tool for legitimate users, like dissidents.

Understanding the best enforcement techniques is just the first step. The United States is constitutionally committed to protecting freedom of expression on the internet in ways that many other countries are not. Some countries wish to have complete control of the traffic on the internet. They see freedom of speech as a threat to their power and the Dark Web as a tool that enables dissidents to speak freely. The internet is by its nature an international network of computers. Enforcement jurisdiction is foggy at best, so governments must find ways to cooperate in establishing at least some mutually agreeable regulations that govern the Dark Web.

The debate surrounding the Dark Web is by no means over. Online anonymity is a double-edged sword that must be handled delicately. As policy-makers move forward, they must monitor vigilantly the evolution of the Dark Web and ensure that enforcement agencies have the resources and legal support to police successfully the Dark Web. Dark Web policy, like all good policy, must be nuanced and thoughtful in order to strike the balance between the needs of privacy-minded users and the government's responsibility to stop illegal activity.

A Global Perspective on the Benefits and Drawbacks of the Dark Web

Summer Lightfoot

Summer Lightfoot is a writer and researcher focused on online privacy, cyber security, and the relationship between technology and human rights. She is a graduate student in the international affairs department at the New School.

[…]

Although the deep web certainly has its dark parts, it also has some incredibly beneficial uses. The media has painted the deep web as something horrible due to the reputation of the Silk Road, but there is a lot more going on besides criminal activity. The deep web can be used for free speech and there are human rights activists, journalists, military, law enforcement as well as normal people on the deep web, it just really depends on what you want to do (NPR). Reformers and political dissidents around the world use the dark web to communicate and build movements for deserving and lawful protest and reform in war-torn areas such as Syria. Tor's early adopters weren't criminals, they were dissidents and one of them is Nima Fatemi, a black-clad 27-year-old Iranian who helped others around the world use the software to fight oppressive regimes. At the beginning of Tor and the deep web's history in the 1990's, it was simply just the hidden part of the internet.

We need places of true anonymity online, as it advances human creativity and protects vital human rights, including the right to free speech and furthermore the deep web offers this. According to Kim Zeeter, a reporter from Wired, there is another purpose that doesn't usually make the news: It helps political dissidents who want to evade government censors and

"Surveillance and Privacy on the Deep Web," by Summer Lightfoot, May 5, 2017. Reprinted by permission.

has become a valuable tool for Chinese dissidents who can't access sites like Twitter. The deep web allows oppressed people to access information their governments would never dream of letting them see, which helps fight ignorance and provides knowledge. In fact, it played a key role in the many revolutions that toppled horrific dictators in the Middle East back in 2011 and "Dr Ian Walden was quoted by Motherboard as saying that the deep web was instrumental in allowing for information to be spread during the Arab Spring" (Roesler). It also helps people that work for governmental agencies or secret organizations reveal confidential and important information that the general public does not know about, such as whistleblowers and reporters.

There are several tasks that are perfectly legal to perform on the deep web, and you might not realize that the data being accessed actually resides there. When somebody performs a background check on an individual, it searches several databases on the Internet for information. This information is actually being searched for on the deep web. Another use for the deep web is if an adopted person wanted to try and search for their natural parents. The databases that house this adoption information are on the deep web. You can also use the deep web to perform veteran research or look up your genealogy history. Legal research is also conducted on the deep web for cases. If you are a student, you can use the deep web too. There are several academic databases that you can search through for topics, such as scientific journals and source material. Victims of digital abuse such as cyberstalking have used the deep web and Tor to protect their personal security and privacy. Companies from all kinds of industries need to be able to access and share private data without the fear of hackers gaining control of it, and the deep web is incredibly good at this. And while its size and complexity make it a powerful knowledge source, the deep web also has a wide variety of offerings that can be adapted to meet business needs such as competitive intelligence, cross-enterprise collaboration, techno-elitism and innovative technology solutions. Many businesses might want to send information without having it traced or get past an advanced firewall and the deep web allows them to do so.

[...]

Privacy and Anonymity on the Deep Web

Anonymity is one of the greatest advantages of the internet and it "...is important for the possibility of democracy...it provides space for people to think and voice opinions that are against the grain...it ensures both protection for an individual that holds a minority point of view and a window of opportunity for the majority consensus to be challenged by outside ways of thinking (Jardine). In non-democratic countries, the presence of anonymity is the only way that people can voice contrary points of view against despotic regimes in the hope of securing political freedom. There is a familiar mantra that all internet users should live by that goes along with maintaining privacy and anonymity, "although it seems users of the dark web may have forgotten three important rules in their haste to experience the illusion of anonymity: nobody is anonymous, anybody can be hacked, and all information can be made public" (Rossi). Martin Roesler, Senior Director of the Trend Micro Forward-Looking Threat Research (FTR) team has said that "Maintaining anonymity in the deep web depends on the user. Because TOR has already become popular, many users tend to neglect certain things they need to do to stay hidden. If you go into the deep web, you'll find a lot of users who still leave their email addresses, making them searchable" (Roesler), meaning that is up to the user and their level of caution to stay safe when accessing the deep web.

In several parts of the world, privacy has developed within the context of human rights and the right to privacy is now essentially the individual's right to have and to maintain control over information about him. In the United States, privacy has focused on the right to privacy of one's person. Unlike the E.U., the US Constitution does not provide a "right" to privacy, whereas European legal texts define privacy as a human right. Furthermore, the US has no single, overarching privacy law. Instead, it follows a sectoral approach that imposes federal regulations on specific industries, such as healthcare and consumer credit reporting, while leaving others unprotected. Beyond these limited federal privacy restrictions, Congress has left stricter privacy legislation to the states. There are several tools outside of Tor that is common knowledge to the public that can be used to secure privacy and anonymity such as Anonymous email and using a Virtual Private Network (VPN) or private search engine. Using Tor alone is not enough to remain secure on the deep web and it has been recommended to use a VPN along with Tor. A major ongoing question has been do we really have privacy online? It is common knowledge when using the internet that there is no privacy because user data is always being collected, but on the deep web, it is assumed that there is complete privacy. If someone wants to buy someone else's private data, it's disturbingly easy to do. It's all there for sale on the dark web, a completely anonymous twin of the web most of us use daily. As seen here, there ultimately is no privacy on the internet. When we access the surface web on a daily basis for social media, Google, email and so on, what we are doing is tracked and collected. The data that is collected is used and sold to make a profit. It does not matter to corporations whether or not we have privacy on the internet because it benefits them if we do not have the privacy of our own data. This is similar to the CIA leaks of March 2017, where Wikileaks released CIA hacking information that showed how much surveillance the CIA has control over. The CIA has software that can hack into smartphones and smart televisions to basically take control of the devices. Government agencies do not want the general public to have privacy because they think by having access to our data can help to keep the nation safe.

Surveillance of the Deep Web

[…]

When it comes to surveillance of terrorism on the deep web, The Foreign Intelligence Surveillance Act (FISA) has defined the contours of the warrant clause of the Fourth Amendment regarding electronic interceptions on US soil "FISA is the primary vehicle allowing the government to conduct covert surveillance of those suspected of terrorist activities in the United States," and allows "for electronic surveillance of communications between or among foreign powers," without a court order, in some circumstances (Dastagir Vogt). In Section 702 of FISA, it allows for broad monitoring of Internet activity by non-US persons believed to be located outside the United States. Government agencies, such as the NSA have been collecting data on people with the argument that it is to keep us safe. With the data that they collect, the NSA will be able to stop crimes before they happen and catch terrorists in the act. This can be done by tracing what a suspected terrorist searches on Google, orders online and where they go. All of this information can be collected from collected data and used to make a case to stop them.

[…]

Conclusion

As we have witnessed time and time again, the deep web is cause for great concern over the safety of our data, privacy and wellbeing. Law enforcement is working to increase its efficiency in surveilling the deep web and catching its criminals. The deep web exists to maintain anonymity on the internet and could be considered a form of peaceful, civil disobedience, depending on what it is used for but if continues to be used in illegal ways, it is clear that law enforcement will have to increase its surveillance of it. Given my analysis, the best way that law enforcement and governmental agencies can do with respect to the deep web is use the systems and analytics that can track and store information from the deep web and "while it's not likely for a majority of Internet users to ever find reasons to use the Dark Web, anonymity in the Deep Web will continue to raise a lot of issues and be a point of interest for both law enforcers and Internet users who want to circumvent government surveillance and intervention" (Ciancaglini et al. 42), as well as terrorist operations. Going forward, many will continue to question how to best handle the ever evolving technology such as encryption and the challenges posed by the terrorists and people who exploit cyberspace, including the deep and dark webs. Despite their efforts, law enforcement agencies should continue to train agents in understanding and mastering the new technologies that make up the deep web. It would also be beneficial for law enforcement to learn the tactics and practices used by deep web criminals, that allow them to get away with their crimes (Cook). If the state continues to monitor the deep web and furthers the development of tools that can track illegal sites and activity. Monitoring and the deep web is the best way counteract against its illegal and criminal uses.

Current
CONTROVERSIES

CHAPTER 2

Is It Possible to Effectively Monitor and Regulate Activity on the Dark Web?

The Dark Web: How Does It Work?

Ed Smith

Ed Smith is a professional writer whose work focuses on web technology and its uses. His writing has appeared in TruthFinder and Infomania.

When you look at the sky, what do you see? A blazing sun, a band of clouds, an occasional airplane. It doesn't look like much, but you know there's more than meets the eye. Beyond your infinitesimal view of the universe are entire galaxies that stretch further than you could ever imagine.

And that's why our colossal universe is a fitting metaphor for the World Wide Web. Both are constantly expanding and changing—and completely misunderstood. No matter how much probing we do, we'll never fully grasp what's out there.

So, before we explore those outer reaches of cyberspace, let's start at ground zero: the origin of the internet.

A Brief History of the World Wide Web

Before the internet, there was the ARPANET, a computer network used by the US government to share sensitive data in the 1970s. About a decade later, the ARPANET's limited networks gave way to a single, worldwide network we call the internet.

However, the internet as we know it didn't materialize until 1991. That's when an English programmer introduced the World Wide Web as a place to store information, not just send and receive it. Gone were the days of only using the internet to send emails or post articles in forums. Now users could create and find web pages for just about anything.

As the World Wide Web grew in popularity, users faced a new problem: learning to navigate it. Along came Google (and its

"What's Hiding in the Dark Web?" by Ed Smith, TruthFinder, July 5, 2018. Reprinted by permission.

predecessors) to give users a starting point for their web search. With the help of search engines, users could finally explore cyberspace without getting completely lost.

Why Google Won't Find Everything

Today's biggest search engines are much more adept than they were 20 years ago. They can predict your search, interpret multi-word inquiries, and serve trillions of (yes, we said trillions) of webpages.

However, despite Google's web prowess, it and other search engines have a very limited view of what's out there. (Some researchers say that search engines only show about 1% of what's actually available online!)

Search engines work by "crawling" links on a website. If a site owner doesn't want a page on their site to be found, it won't include a direct link to that page. If a web page has no link, it can't be crawled or indexed in Google's massive search library. The page won't appear as a result on a search engine.

The Surface Web

Because search engines skim the surface of what's available online, the websites they show on their results pages are part of what's called the Surface Web. Using Google is like scanning the horizon with your naked eye. Sure, there's a lot to take in, but you're only seeing a tiny bit of what's happening in the world.

The Deep Web

When you find web pages that a typical search engine can't access, you're using the Deep Web. We know the *Deep Web* sounds intimidating, but believe it or not, you use it every day. When you search for a place on Airbnb, or compare plane flights on Expedia, you're using the Deep Web. When you log in to your email account, online bank account, or Amazon account, you're using the Deep Web.

Anytime you log in to an account, or search for information directly on a web page, you're getting access to Deep Web content that won't show up on a search engine. And that's a good thing. If someone Googled your name, you wouldn't want your banking information or Amazon wish list showing up in results. That information is meant to be private, so those sensitive web pages aren't crawled by search engines.

Using the Deep Web is like looking at the world from an airplane. At such high elevations, you'll have a much broader vantage point than your friends on Earth.

How to Access the Deep Web

It's easy. Just go to TruthFinder, type in someone's name, and press enter. The results that show up come from TruthFinder's database of Deep Web sources.

Google will redirect you to public records search engines like TruthFinder, but it won't show you specific public records related to the name you're searching. Those records are held by local, state, and federal databases that Google can't show in search results. To get to that database of public records, you have to actually search a third-party provider, like TruthFinder.

Here's another example of the difference between Surface and Deep Web content: Before I published this blog post, I saved it as a draft on WordPress. The article existed as a web page on WordPress, but you weren't able to find it. Technically, that draft was part of the Deep Web. Once I posted this piece to Infomania, Google could crawl the page link I published. Since the piece now pulls up in search results, it's considered Surface Web content.

The Dark Web

The Dark Web still falls under the Deep Web umbrella; it's just a much, much smaller portion of the Deep Web. The Dark Web, or "Darknet," uses masked IP address to intentionally hide web pages from search engines, web page search forms, and even standard web browsers. In fact, according to Andy Greenberg at *Wired*, the Dark Web accounts for less than .01% of the Deep Web.

The Deep Web is the part of cyberspace that only a small proportion of internet users will ever access. If the typical internet browser has a view from the ground or an airplane, the Deep Web user has a view from space. They're the astronauts of the internet, the ones with the most expansive vantage point to the internet universe.

How to Access the Dark Web

Dark Web sites are so bent on anonymity, they require a special web browser to access them.

The majority of Dark Web sites in America use the TOR Network (short for The Onion Router). A TOR network is a collection of "volunteer" computer networks that send users' encrypted traffic to multiple servers before pulling up content. That way, a user's browsing session is so jumbled up, their identity and location is almost untraceable.

The Good, the Bad, and the Downright Ugly of the Dark Web

Because the TOR network allows users to browse anonymously, it's used by secret service agents, law enforcement, activists, researchers, whistleblowers, and users who are banned from Internet access.

WikiLeaks is a notorious Dark Web site that allows whistleblowers to anonymously upload classified information to the press. While the legality of leaking classified information is a hot topic in the US, no formal charges have been made against WikiLeaks founder, Julian Assange. (He does, however, have an arrest warrant for allegations of rape and molestation against two women in 2010.)

Even Facebook has a Dark Web site. Last October, the social media giant launched a Tor hidden service so users could avoid surveillance or censorship.

Anonymity, however, has a dark side. The TOR network can also be used to hide the identities of users involved in criminal activity.

Here are the types of illegal operations you could find on the TOR network:

- Sale of unlicensed firearms
- Child pornography
- Sale of malware, pirated software, and hacking guides
- Sale of illegal drugs
- Identity hacks and sale of stolen credit card information and user accounts
- Sale of forged documents and currency
- Hiring hit men
- Gambling
- Money laundering
- Insider trading

The Silk Road is the best-known source of nefarious activity on the Dark Web. Known as the "Amazon of drugs," the site sold high-grade, illegal drugs—that is, until it got shut down by the FBI. Evolution, Agora Marketplace, and Nucleus Marketplace are three additional examples of popular black market sites.

Get the Best View with a Deep Web Search

Now that we've covered all of cyberspace, here's a short recap of the depths you can go online:

1. The Surface Web: Web pages that show up on search engine results. If you can find it on a Google search, it's typically part of the Surface Web.

2. The Deep Web: All content that a search engine can't access. Deep Web pages include information protected by a login, a website database, or a page that doesn't have a link.

3. The Dark Web: A small, anonymous niche of the Deep Web that's intentionally hidden from search engines. It requires a special web browser for users to access it.

Next time you do a Google search, keep in mind that you're seeing a very limited version of what's available in cyberspace. Sure, you'll be glad you can't see it all. But if you want the best view of what's out there, you need access to databases that Google can't show.

Start searching the Deep Web today with a TruthFinder membership. You'll be able to uncover details about almost anyone (including yourself) pulled directly from public records, including property ownership, social media profiles, location history, and even criminal records.

You can also use TruthFinder to keep tabs on your personal information with Dark Web Monitoring. Data breaches are becoming more and more common in the digital age, and your sensitive information will sell to the highest bidder on the Dark Web.

That means your credit card info, medical ID numbers, and even Social Security numbers are all vulnerable—but with Dark Web Monitoring, you'll find out instantly if your data is compromised. Then, you can take action to protect yourself before your identity falls into the wrong hands.

Dark Web Crawling Is a Viable Law Enforcement Technique

Jacob Koshy

Jacob Koshy is a content marketer and technology writer. In his current position with PromptCloud, he develops data extraction techniques for private sector enterprises.

You might think that you have full access to the internet, but the truth is your access is limited to the tip of an iceberg that the web really is. Search engines like google can only access the surface web, which makes up to about .03 percent of the whole web. The rest is called dark web aka deep web and is a mysterious place. Nobody really knows exactly how big it is, but is estimated to be about 500 to 6000 times larger than the surface web. Curious about taking a look at the deep web? You can't, with your regular browser. You will require a special browser to enter deep web, and there, you are completely anonymous.

This secret world is also infamous for being the breeding ground of cyber and real world crimes. The main reason is obviously the anonymity that it provides. Illegal activities like drug trade, counterfeit currency dealings, weapons and ammunition trade, forgery and even hitmen services lurk behind the shadows of this anonymity.

How It Works

The dark web is basically the shadiest corners of the web where search engines don't go. People interact there without the watchful eyes of government authorities. These sites are typically encrypted with mechanisms like Tor that lets users visit them while staying anonymous. For the same reason, it is being used by criminals to carry out illegal activities without getting tracked in any way.

"How Crawling the Dark Web Can Help Curb Crime," by Jacob Koshy, PromptCloud, December 9, 2016. Reprinted by permission.

Tor works like an onion, hence the onion logo of the Tor browser. This means, when you go behind an IP address that accessed a particular website, you will simply find more layers of IP addresses. The real IP address of the user cannot be traced back, just like you wouldn't find anything if you keep peeling off onion skins. Many websites, especially the ones into illegal things can only be accessed via the Tor browser. The transactions in the dark web are done via bitcoin, which makes it almost impossible to track like the regular credit card transactions.

Types of Crime on the Dark Web

There is a wide variety of crimes being carried out with the help of dark web. Here are some examples:

Cyber Fraud

Dark web is the breeding ground of methods and processes for stealing credit card data and personal information. Criminals first break into merchant sites or payment gateways to steal the card data and then sell it off to other scammers who run card forums and market sites. Batches of card details are finally laundered for cash via this process. Sales of new computer exploits is also among the biggest threats in the dark web. Once the exploit has been sold to more hackers, the scale of the attack becomes large.

Real World Crimes

Many real-world crimes have been associated with dark web for a long time now. Silk Road was one of the first darknets that hosted the sales of illegal drugs until 2013 when it was shut down by the FBI. Many darknets have sprung up to take the place of Silk Road after that. It's likely that any illegal drug that you can name would be available to buy on some darknet in the deep web. Drug mafias use courier systems to transport these drugs to the clients stealthily which makes it a hard menace to control.

Sales of weapons have seen rise and fall on the deep web. For instance, there have been many high-profile arrests in the UK that has made the cyber criminals see arms trafficking as a high-risk business. Many sites on the dark web still sell rocket launchers, tanks, firearms and other highly dangerous explosives. Apart from this, hitmen are available to hire, human organs are being trafficked and even terrorist attacks are being planned on some of the deep web sites out there.

Web Crawling to Curb the Dark Web Crimes

Web crawling technologies are increasing in popularity among the business users for its incredible power to provide competitive intelligence and fuel extensive web research. We believe that the crawling technologies can be applied to darknets on the deep web in order to curb this growing menace of crime through web. Here are some ways crawling can help.

Detecting Potentially Illegal Content

Not all of deep web or even the .onion sites are into crimes or anything illegal in nature. Given the huge size of the deep web, it won't be feasible for the authorities to manually visit each site and evaluate its content for a potentially illegal nature. This is where crawling comes in. Web crawling can be used to crawl and index millions of such sites in short notice and can even be programmed to report when certain keywords are detected. These keywords could be anything to watch out for say, names of guns, drugs—a set of words that's associated with illegal activities on the deep web. This makes finding things on the darknets easier and now the only job left is to track the criminals behind these illegal activities. To begin with, this is quite a challenging task given how everything is anonymous on the dark web. It's not impossible though, that's how FBI caught Ross Ulbricht, the founder of Silk Road—one of the first criminal marketplaces on the dark web.

Tracing Down the Bitcoin

All the hype apart, Bitcoin is not as anonymous as it may seem to be. It's basically electronic cash and like all things digital, it does leave trails behind. Though bitcoin is never associated with personal details of the holders, every bitcoin transaction is recorded in a public log with their wallet IDs. This means, bitcoin is only safe as long as you are super careful with it. One bad move and the user could be booked with all the necessary evidence. By connecting the dots between individual transactions using machine learning, we could even expect better tracking mechanisms to identify bitcoin holders in the near future. With web crawling technologies, the bitcoin logs can be continuously monitored for cues that can lead to a connection.

Identifying Zero Day Attacks

Dark web is where all the new vulnerabilities in computer systems get released first, in the form of exploits and malware. In February 2015, Microsoft identified a serious vulnerability in the windows operating system. Although they immediately released a fix, the details of the vulnerability spread through the dark web like wildfire. Hackers are actively looking for vulnerabilities like this to turn into an exploit and sell it off on the dark web.

This is why Eric Nunes and pals at the Arizona State University came up with a hybrid of web crawling and machine learning technologies that can crawl the hacking forums on the dark web for early detection of security vulnerabilities. This can effectively help in fixing them at the earliest to prevent huge cyber-attacks.

Prevention of Real World Crimes

Real world crimes are planned, assigned and paid for on the dark web. This includes terrorist forums and darknets where people are offered incentives to take part in attacks and are recruited directly. In fact, this is a challenging task to accomplish as anonymous communication happens on the dark web. But, the likes of terrorist attacks could be predicted by mining data and using predictive modelling techniques on forums where discussions of that nature happen. By using web crawling to monitor the darknet sites, it is possible to get hints about such attacks and take preventive measures.

Technology is neither good nor bad, it is the users who make it act in either directions. While being used for illegal activities mostly, the technologies that work behind it aren't inherently good or bad. As the number of crimes using technology is on the rise, nothing but technology can be used to put an end to it. Since machine learning technologies are improving by each passing day, we can soon expect a combination of web data mining and machine learning to help curb the menace of dark web crimes.

The Dark Web Presents Challenges and Opportunities for Law Enforcement

Katie A. Paul

Katie A. Paul is a journalist whose work focuses on technology and business in the Middle East. Her writing has appeared in the Los Angeles Times, Foreign Affairs, *the* Daily Beast, *and the* New Republic. *She currently works on the Arabian Peninsula desk at Reuters.*

A rt and antiquities are often a frequent target of theft, looting, and trafficking by organized criminals and violent extremists. The grey nature of the art market allows for antiquities to be easily laundered through online sales, falsified documentation, and underground person-to-person trade. Terrorist groups such as the Islamic State of Iraq and Syria (ISIS, also known as Daesh and ISIL) have used the trafficking of illicit antiquities from the Middle East and North Africa as a source of financing since shortly after the group's rise to power in 2014. The rise of antiquities trafficking by terror groups has prompted the US Federal Bureau of Investigation (FBI) to issue a formal warning to dealers and collectors to take extra care in their due diligence of Middle Eastern artifacts. The recognition of illicit cultural property a terror financing threat that has also precipitated policy moves from the United States and the European Commission.

While other transnational criminal groups, such as the Haqqani network in Pakistan, and even Italian mafia have been identified as agents of art and antiquities trafficking, the highly advanced technological maneuvering of ISIS's overall operations has placed them in a new level of threats in the digital realm. The group has sustained their operations through recruitment, extortion, and

"Ancient Artifacts vs. Digital Artifacts: New Tools for Unmasking the Sale of Illicit Antiquities on the Dark Web," by Katie A. Paul, Arts, March 26, 2018, https://www.mdpi.com/2076-0752/7/2/12/html. Licensed under CC BY 4.0 International.

trafficking of antiquities and more on social networking outlets such as Facebook, Twitter, Telegram, and WhatsApp. However, more concerning are the communications and transactions that cannot be traced as ISIS has delved deeper into the Dark Web.

The elusive nature of dark, encrypted, and untraceable online technologies is an appeal for anyone looking to hide illicit activities—it is also a significant obstacle for authorities seeking to track the actors engaging in illicit behavior. Europol's 2015 report, *Exploring Tomorrow's Organised Crime*, found a connection between the use of cryptocurrencies and illicit trade by organized criminal networks on the Dark Web. The report found that "virtual currencies have already had a significant impact on various types of criminal activity facilitating the exchange of funds between criminal actors and giving rise to a flourishing black-market economy on Darknet marketplaces" (Europol 2015, p. 31). Europol found that the core feature of anonymity in cryptocurrencies and overall Dark Web usage would create difficulty in tracking illegal transactions and cyber activity. "Bitcoin laundering services … will make transactions practically untraceable, heavily facilitating the trade in illicit goods online" (Europol 2015, p. 27). However, new studies have revealed that criminal activities online may not be entirely untraceable after all.

Digital artifacts, sometimes referred to as software artifacts, are by-products of data, digitally linked to specific users, that are left behind from their activity on the Internet. Digital artifacts may be remaining pieces of information created during installation or usage of software. Even Blockchain supported technologies such as the Bitcoin public exchange can leave behind these pieces of digital data, and with Bitcoin becoming a popular currency of antiquities dealers and online criminal groups alike, the grey lines in legitimacy of art market transactions become increasingly blurred.

By scanning online forums and communications networks for key antiquities trafficking terms, heritage experts and authorities can begin crawling the Deep Web and the Dark Web for digital artifacts related to illicit online activities. These artifacts can be sourced from information left from any number of Deep and Dark Web sources, from transactions through cryptocurrency to communications on encrypted messaging apps. Combining methodologies of new cyber forensics with those used to track similar illicit online trades such as wildlife, authorities may be able to get a better understanding of the reach of online antiquities trafficking networks and develop targeted strategies to combat them.

Terrorists' Love Affair with Bitcoin

While ISIS is best known for its outward manipulation of the Surface Web—that is the web that people can access on any given day using search engines such as Google—their shifting movements into both the Deep Web and Dark Web have made their illicit activities difficult to track. The Deep Web (as opposed to the surface web) is all the pieces of unindexed information that will not show up in any of the pages generated by Google. This is the majority of information that is actually on the Internet, but typically inaccessible unless special browsers or web crawling software are used. By contrast, the Dark Web is a small portion of the Deep Web that has been hidden intentionally to maintain anonymity by users.

While both the Deep and Dark Web have a role in illicit cyber activity, the Dark Web has significant appeal to violent extremist groups such as ISIS due to the ability to mask identification. Dark Web surfers often use a Tor browser, which allows for the masking of their IP address—an attractive feature for individuals engaging in illicit trade.

In 2015, following the terror attacks in Paris, ISIS moved many of their communications and recruiting operations to the Deep Web and the Dark Web to avoid hacktivists (activist hackers) trying to infiltrate their networks. The result has led to a largely untraceable network of communication, prime conditions for more openly trafficking artifacts, weapons, and other illicit materials online. In fact, the weapon used for the deadly July 2016 Munich attack is believed to have been purchased on the Dark Web, less than one year after the Paris attacks that expedited violent extremists' online operations shift to the Dark Web.

ISIS had reason to be worried about online tracking. Following the attacks in Paris, GhostSec, an offshoot of the global network of hacktivists known as Anonymous, digitally targeted the terror group revealing the discovery of a Bitcoin wallet in excess of $3 million. The use of Bitcoin for funding by ISIS goes beyond Munich. In 2015, a U.S.-based ISIS cell was soliciting Bitcoin through online networks. In the three years since, the broader use of cryptocurrency globally has vastly expanded, with the Bitcoin market—while volatile—continuing to remain on the overall incline.

But why does this matter?

Since the hacktivism breach by GhostSec, ISIS has had time to maneuver through the depths of the Dark Web—giving them ample headway to mask their communication, trafficking, and financing. The group is known from media reports of their march of destruction and looting across the Middle East to establish their caliphate, but they have lost significant ground since their rise in 2014. However, the danger of ISIS is not limited to their regional territories.

The threat of a digitally-globalized caliphate, one that transcends the physical national boundaries where the group held territory, makes ISIS virtually impossible to fully eradicate. While militants attempt to regroup forces on the ground, their followers and financiers can hide in the shadows of the Dark Web, manipulating more covert opportunities for recruitment and funding. With the wildly popular rise of Bitcoin and other cryptocurrencies, the group's available vehicles for funding become more complex and even more difficult to trace.

The anonymous and unalterable nature of Bitcoin is made possible through Blockchain technology. The attraction of Bitcoin and other cryptocurrencies lies in the anonymity attached to the transactions through the untraceable online wallet. "Darknet markets, by hiding the identities of those involved in transactions and often conducting business via Bitcoin, inherently represent illegality and regulatory evasion. As demonstrated by the Silk Road drug market and its successors, a massive number of Darknet transactions involve contraband" (Sui et al. 2015, p. 10).

For terrorist groups and other criminals an untraceable and unregulated currency that can be accessed from anywhere in the world has obvious benefits. Pair this currency with the veil provided by the Dark Web and criminals have a seemingly impenetrable digital playground for illicit activity.

Art and More on the Dark Web

There is precedence for the illicit trade of more than just drugs and guns online. Illicit wildlife sales, a black market similar and often connected to that in antiquities, have been occurring on the Dark Web for years. In 2017, INTERPOL Global Complex for Innovation in collaboration with International Fund for Animal Welfare (IFAW), the U.S. Department of State, and the African Wildlife Foundation (AWF) identified an illegal market for wildlife and ivory on the Dark Web, with some sale offerings reportedly dating back to 2015. The research project revealed that the primary means of transactions for these illegal offerings were Bitcoin and other cryptocurrencies. Further studies have used what information is accessible to researchers to identify markets and key terms for wildlife trafficking on the Dark Web.

In J.T. Jackman's 2014 book *Bitcoin for Beginners: How to Buy Bitcoins, Sell Bitcoins, and Invest in Bitcoins,* he specifically mentions untraceable illegal antiquities auctions as one of the markets that could be lured by the appeals of Bitcoin as a currency for criminal activity. "There are those who view the anonymity of Bitcoin is a definite "pro" for many. Unfortunately, that includes the "bad guys" of the world too. After all, there is zero "paper trail" behind the use of it … So, it makes it easy for the criminally minded to conduct all kinds of activities—from selling drugs to auctioning antiquities on illegal underground sites" (Jackman 2014, p. 49).

While much of the information on the Dark Web, including networks behind Darknet Markets (DNM), is difficult to maneuver or inaccessible to researchers and law enforcement, recent reports have revealed that the trafficking of illicit art and antiquities are among the many types of transactions taking place.

An October 2017 report from the Wall Street Journal stated that authorities have indicated they are seeing an increase in the sale of illicit antiquities on the Dark Web. However, this is not the first mention of this illicit commodity appearing in the online markets of this shady network—two years ago, a user on the social network and communication forum Reddit, with the username "keepen_it_one_hunnid," claimed in an online discussion about Dark Web access to have seen first-hand the sale of black-market antiquities and many other illicit materials on underground sites.

> "I have personally seen for sale: Fake passports/I.D. packages, cloned credit cards/ fake visa gift cards, long standing eBay accounts with positive ratings, hacking services, wet work, foreign knock-offs of any product imaginable (cell phones, laptops, coats, purses, watches, etc.) Counterfeit art and jewelry, black market antiquities, exotic animals, ivory/ rhino horn/ shark fins, counterfeit money … Really anything that you could think of."
>
> —keepen_it_one_hunnid 2015

Although a seemingly obscure source, reddit has been used to identify networks in illegal wildlife trafficking on the Dark Web. A 2016 study on Dark Web markets specifically listed sources in subreddit as the basis for identifying code words used by networks in illegal wildlife trafficking. These code words were then run though many of the underground online marketplaces to identify offerings of illicit wildlife.

Known stolen art has also already shown up on the Dark Web. In November 2017, a 133-year-old painting that had been stolen from the International Art Centre in New Zealand on 1 April 2017 appeared for auction on the Dark Web auction site known as White Shadow. The seller, listed as "Diablo," offered the painting with the description, "Here you can bid on an [sic] TOP SECRET original Painting from Bohemian painter Gottfried Lindauer that was stolen in New Zealand, Auckland 2017." While the authenticity of the painting has been debated by experts, the piece still sought to pull in hundreds of thousands of dollars.

The stolen painting's listing online had it offered for $350,000— all to be paid in Bitcoin. In addition, while this particular piece was not stolen by ISIS, the incident is notable for the clear connections between stolen art and cryptocurrency on the Dark Web.

ISIS has also been reported to have sold illicit antiquities on the Dark Web by using Bitcoin as an untraceable source of transactions. Haroon Ullah identified a member of ISIS who went by the name of Javaid. The ISIS recruit detailed how he would move antiquities looted from Iraq and Syria by first identifying buyers through social media, specifically connecting to interested buyers in North America and Europe. He would then secure the transactions through sites on the Dark Web, accepting Bitcoin as payment for the pieces. "That was the key: black-market sales using digital cash, with no footprints left behind" (Ullah 2018, p. 174).

This is not the only mention of ISIS selling illicit artifacts for Bitcoin on the Dark Web. Jan Peter Hammer, director of the "Art of War" research project, also encountered a journalist who reported that ISIS was allegedly using Bitcoin for all Dark Web transactions of looted antiquities. Artifacts looted from territories with large terrorist and transnational criminal presence, such as Iraq, Syria, and Yemen, are commonly smuggled through transit routes in Turkey and the Gulf States and then on to Europe, with valuable pieces often held in free ports for years.

The use of free ports to hide artifacts is not a new tactic in the era of ISIS. In 2016, Swiss authorities seized a trove of artifacts that had been looted from Yemen, Syria, and Libya and found in a Swiss free port where they had been sitting since 2009 and 2010.

Many of these valuable pieces that are smuggled out of the Middle East and North Africa have not yet surfaced on the public market and likely will not for ten years or more, particularly those that may be laying low in free ports. Hito Steyerl referred to free ports as "a museum of the Internet era, but a museum of the dark net, where movement is obscured, and data-space is clouded" (Steyerl 2015). We are only at the beginning of the effects of this underground trade online and its implications for the smuggling and laundering of artifacts in the real world.

[…]

Tracing the "Untraceable"

Although Blockchain, the technology behind online currencies such as Bitcoin, and the concept of a digital currency that is untamperable and unregulated has been criticized for the opportunities it may present to criminals and terrorist groups, it should be noted that this technology also holds new potential for cyber security investigations, including efforts in the fight against terrorism and trafficking.

Blockchain technology allows for the creation of digital records or tags that cannot be altered or tampered with. The permanent and unchanging nature of the digital records that can be created by Blockchain technologies present opportunities in the protection of artifacts against illicit trade while addressing some of the vulnerabilities of existing documentations. In addition to its more well-known applications to cryptocurrency, Blockchain technology can be used for the creation of title deeds and smart contacts. Like land, antiquities and other cultural property elements can be treated in the same manner as Bitcoin, with Blockchain technology used to assign a smart contract (also known as a cryptocontract) to the owner of the piece—in the case of registered antiquities, the ownership would go to a national government or museum.

While Blockchain technology holds potential to create valuable records that can help combat the illicit antiquities trade and increase the legitimacy of artifacts on the legal market, online illicit trafficking networks are moving more quickly than the infrastructure and capacity of cultural heritage institutions can keep up with. Understanding how criminals are using the Dark Web, cryptocurrency, and masking software is of critical importance to expedite law enforcement efforts to shut off a vein of the illicit antiquities trade that has yet to be fully explored.

Legally, options to pursue the illicit actors on the Dark Web who may manipulate transaction opportunities using Bitcoin are few. The regulatory environment in illicit cyber activity is still in the very early stages of development. However, new monitoring mechanisms are constantly evolving.

The rise of the usage of cryptocurrency may open new doors to tracking financial movements of terrorist organizations, transnational trafficking networks, and other illicit online actors— including those trafficking in art and antiquities. Cryptocurrencies leave behind artifacts of their own—digital artifacts—which can be traced to identify the online activity of otherwise "untraceable" users. Much in the same way that pieces of websites, articles, sales, and more can be found through crawling the Deep Web, pieces of cryptocurrency transactions from the public exchange and elsewhere can also be identified. "These evidentiary artifacts, whether a timestamp, an electronic document or e-mail provides a digital case with the solid foundation it needs in order to hold up in the eyes of the court" (Doran 2015). Digital web crawling tools such as Internet Evidence Finder (IEF) or cyber intelligence platform Sixgill can recover artifacts left behind by Bitcoin transactions, social media activity, email accounts and more, opening the door to tracking illicit cyber activity. Cyber forensics experts use web crawling software and intelligence platforms such as these to gather evidence from laptops, computers, and online accounts, in the form of digital artifacts.

Using the Sixgill cyber intelligence platform for a preliminary search of illicit antiquities and cultural property on the Dark Web, digital artifacts of Telegram communications revealed that jihadi networks are indeed illicitly trading coins and artifacts. Digital artifacts, discovered using the Sixgill web crawling technology, from a Telegram chat group known for trafficking communications among jihadi and militant users, included photos and even phone numbers of the offending traffickers.

These coins and small artifacts being offered in this particular Telegram group were posted in February 2018. The primary communications in this group were composed of Islamist propaganda and trafficking in coins, artifacts, and weapons. The platform also includes a tag for the "weapons" that Sixgill had assigned to this Telegram group.

New analysis from researchers at Qatar University in January 2018 revealed that they were able to link publicly available information on the Blockchain, social media, and Deep Web sites with the transactions of Bitcoin users on the Dark Web, resulting in the unmasking over 125 Tor users. The Qatar University team was able to trace back transactions for years, meaning even the early days of Bitcoin purchases, such as those that were made on the online black-market drug site Silk Road, can be traced.

Applying a similar methodology to that used in identification of the illegal wildlife trade by Harrison et al. on the Dark Web—that is the scanning of Dark Web and Deep Web discussion forums for key terminology to use in Dark Web crawling—may yield results in uncovering the black-market art and antiquities trade online. By searching comments on subreddit, interest in—and experience with—Dark Web art and antiquities can be easily found. The subreddit for Dark Net Markets (r/DarkNetMarkets) reveals one user who goes by the name "storytimeppl" with a specific request for Chinese and Egyptian artifacts—he later responds to a commenter about the benefits of using Bitcoin for transactions in this space. Posts such as these can help identify the period and origin of cultural property that Dark Web users are seeking. In an October 2017 post for the subreddit Darknet (r/Darknet), redditor "tery_mac" sought a "DNM" (abbreviation for Darknet market) in stolen goods—when asked what he was seeking he specifically noted "paintings, artifacts and rare stuff" (tery_mac 2017).

Dark Web markets are not the only place redditors are seeking advice on finding antiquities. The Deep Web is also a subject of discussion. A user—who has since deleted their Reddit account—posted in the Deep Web subreddit (r/deepweb) seeking an antiquities dealer in October 2017. While such a broad request may seem harmless, seeking the dealer in a subreddit for the Deep Web likely means they are deliberately looking to get items outside of the public legitimate market.

Redditors are not just interested in artifacts and paintings on the Dark Web, there is also interest in smaller portable objects, such as coins, which have even less regulation and oversight than the overall art and antiquities market. Reddit user "highcubist" openly requested markets for coins and other old objects in November 2017 in a subreddit meant for antiques. The redditor noted that he has seen counterfeit items thus far but is interested in the "real deal" (highcubist 2017a). The same redditor went even further with his requests in December 2017 when his interests in illicit ancient material evolved. He asked specifically for Middle Eastern antiquities, with the caveat that he was not interested in provenance, "Have friends interested in Middle Eastern antiquities, do you know of anything available? Not concerned about provenance and origin. Would be happy to discuss a finder's fee" (highcubist 2017b).

The requests by highcubist are of interest due to their specificity for Middle Eastern antiquities and disregard for provenance. Using the Sixgill platform, a query for the screen name "highcubist" was entered to identify any digital artifacts where this user may have engaged elsewhere—and he has. Two posts by a screenname for "highcubist" were found where he was seeking information through discussion forums on the Dark Web regarding coins and artifacts available on DNMs. These posts occur around the same general timeframe as the reddit posts by the same screen name, indicating that they are likely to be the same individual due to the atypical screen name and the nature of the requests.

While some art and antiquities market experts have been skeptical of the existence of a Dark Web market for artifacts, the surge of reddit requests for leads on this market in late 2017 would suggest interests of Dark Web users have changed. With reddit serving as a public forum, and commentary accessible even without the security of a reddit account, the comments posted to date show a clear interest in specifically illicit and Deep and Dark Web markets for antiquities as well as interest in unprovenanced items.

Conclusions

Monitoring and intervention of the illicit antiquities trade on the Deep Web and the Dark Web would not only serve to intercept financial sources for violent extremists and organized criminals, but also to address the burgeoning black market for illicit antiquities which has high demand in Western countries including the United States. The highly sophisticated and globalized nature of cybercrime today forces authorities to continue to modify and update their activities in response to these crimes.

Advancements in Blockchain technology, web crawling software, and monitoring and intelligence gathering methodologies are proving more successful for authorities who are continuing to remove black-market Dark Web sites from the Internet, but significant gaps still exist in the types of black-market networks being monitored. The illicit antiquities trade is one of those gaps.

The "Illegal Wildlife Trade in the Darknet" research report released by the INTERPOL Global Complex for Innovation in collaboration with International Fund for Animal Welfare (IFAW), the US Department of State, and the African Wildlife Foundation (AWF) shows there are opportunities for the Department of State and INTERPOL to deploy their web crawling and cyber security tools for the monitoring of black-market trade online—with a focus on the extent of Dark Web trafficking of antiquities and the types of actors engaged in these crimes.

In response to the reported findings of INTERPOL's Dark Web study on wildlife, the organization launched a special training course on digital forensics of wildlife investigations. With many parallels between the black-market trade in wildlife and antiquities, a training course on identification of illicit cultural property could be incorporated into INTERPOL's digital forensics efforts to dually combat these often-interconnected trades.

By targeting transactions in art and antiquities using the methodologies applied to other illegal online trades, authorities can fill a gap in our understanding of the demographics of black-market traders. Unmasking some of the world's most sophisticated cyber-traffickers of cultural property and opening doors to understanding the next generation of this rapidly evolving illicit trade.

Although Challenging, Patrolling the Dark Web Is Possible and Essential

Shawn R. Kehoe

Shawn R. Kehoe is a lieutenant with the fraud and cyber crimes bureau of the Los Angeles County Sheriff's Department.

The world is an interconnected society, with information traveling at the speed of electrons.[1] Over 40 percent of the world population is connected to the Internet—nearly 3.7 billion people—making it a vital thread in the fabric of society.[2] Social networking, digital news, and e-commerce on the Internet are the norm. It might be surprising to consider that the first Internet browser was invented in 1990—less than 30 years ago.[3] In 1995, less than 1 percent of the world's population accessed the Internet.[4] At that time, no one could have imagined how transformative the Internet would be to society. Considering that many current law enforcement executives were of working-age by the time the Internet was in widespread use, it is easy to see how criminal activity on the Internet and law enforcement's capability to combat cybercrime are apparently out of sync.

The Internet allows one to be interconnected via information and perception, but simultaneously disconnected from direct human observation. This form of human interaction provides a degree of anonymity. With this anonymity, though, comes the risk of increased criminal behavior—creating a realm of crime that poses geographical and technological problems for law enforcement.[5] Many of these crimes emerge from the "dark web," so the first necessary step is that law enforcement understand what the dark web is and how it impacts law enforcement's attempts to control online crimes. The dark web is a confusing place shrouded by anonymity, akin to an alleyway in a gang-ridden

"The Digital Alleyway: Why the Dark Web Cannot Be Ignored," by Shawn R. Kehoe, International Association of Chiefs of Police, June 12, 2018. Reprinted by permission.

neighborhood—a common site of crime hidden from plain sight. Yet, unlike an alleyway that is actively patrolled by law enforcement, the police rarely drive down this "digital alleyway."

The Digital Alleyway

There are around 4 billion websites indexed on Internet search engines and accessible to the average user.[6] These websites are on a part of the Internet most people interact with daily, known as the surface web. The deep web, on the other hand, consists of areas of the Internet not easily accessible on a browser. This includes virtual private networks, corporate databases, and websites not directly linked to the surface web. It is estimated the deep web is considerably larger than the surface web—by 400 to 500 times. Only .2 percent of the Internet is estimated to be on the surface web; the other 99.8 percent of Internet data resides on the deep web.[7]

Within the deep web resides the dark web.[8] The dark web consists of a highly encrypted network, with websites hidden from standard search engines. It is accessible via The Onion Router (TOR) web browser engine, developed in 2002, using a variety of hidden servers to access these sites. Moreover, it is unknown how many users access the dark web.[9] Due to the anonymity and encryption it offers, the dark web is often associated with criminal activity on the Internet. The most famous site that brought widespread attention to the dark web was Silk Road, an illegal drug marketplace. The founder, Ross Ulbricht, was ultimately arrested and sentenced to life in prison in 2013; however, the publicity of the case actually caused the dark web to expand. For example, the Silk Road had approximately 12,000 illegal drugs listed in 2013, but the now-closed Alphabay had more than 300,000 listings in 2017.[10]

Despite its rapid growth, the dark web remains a mysterious place to the majority of the population.[11] It is often sensationalized on television with a focus on scare tactics.[12] Unfortunately, this same limited level of understanding exists for a significant proportion of law enforcement professionals.[13] Although many large agencies employ some components of cybercrime investigation and the topic has been discussed at law enforcement conferences, very few agencies actively monitor and take enforcement actions on the dark web. This can be attributed to a lack of resources and technical expertise, as well as an overall deficit of understanding.[14] Criminals recognize and capitalize on law enforcement's reluctance to enter the dark web, allowing the emergence of crimes that police are not prepared to monitor or combat.

Current Implications for Law Enforcement

Since the beginning of the Internet, the surface web has been used to commit criminal activity. Websites such as Craigslist and Backpage have been linked to crimes such as human trafficking, robbery, and murder.[15] Even today, there is still a great deal of illegal activity committed on the surface web; however, once law enforcement becomes aware of it, an investigation leading to an arrest often occurs. One does not need to look any further for such an example than the seizure and ultimate closure of Backpage by the US Department of Justice.[16] This is because many users of the surface web lack the technical sophistication necessary to hide their identities on the Internet.

On the dark web, however, Internet Service Providers (ISP) do not have the ability to directly monitor web traffic, and the TOR engine is designed for the sole purpose of encryption and anonymity.[17] It is nearly impossible to locate the dark website a criminal used to commit a crime.[18] As a result, criminal activity on the dark web is often very difficult to identify and track, let alone gather enough information to obtain a conviction.[19]

Unlike visible criminal activity on the street, the anonymous nature of the dark web and inherent jurisdictional issues limit the ability of law enforcement to identify the cause or nexus to the dark web. Law enforcement deals with a wide variety of crimes ranging from violent assault to complex identity theft. Often, the focus is on the fruits of the crime or the end results. As an example, a stolen firearm discovered during a traffic stop is tracked as a crime, yet the fact the firearm was bought and sold through the dark web may never be discovered or captured in statistics. Identifying the causation and nexus of criminal activity, however, is vitally important, and could lead to an overall reduction of criminal behavior. This can be seen when targeting gang neighborhoods or areas with visible drug or human trafficking problems, which results in an overall reduction of criminal activity.[20] Without active enforcement on the dark web, criminals are motivated and incentivized to continue committing their crimes on the dark web.

Statistics show an average growth of overall first-use Internet users of 12.75 percent per year, over the past 10 years.[21] This statistic, along with increased encryption for the dark web and an overall acceptance of the dark web's existence by the younger generation, signals a significant potential for increased growth of the dark web in the coming years.[22] The creators of TOR, the gateway to the dark web, are seeking to dispel the "dark" elements of the dark web and increase the number of average daily users.[23] This makes criminal investigations on the dark web even more difficult, as the dark web becomes filled with users on the dark web doing relatively innocent things, without realizing that sharks are swimming with them. Law enforcement agencies must adapt to this expansion and be prepared to actively patrol the dark web. In addition to increasing cybercrime-related budgets, additional training, staffing, and job classifications should be considered when it comes to dark web enforcement.

Recommendations

As public awareness grows, and the media continues to sensationalize the dark web, there will be increased public demand to combat criminal cyber activity.[24] Law enforcement executives have the ability, though, to champion a new direction when it comes to the dark web. Every agency, from large to small, can do their part, even if they are not large enough to have a dedicated unit to investigate crimes on the Internet. There are three areas to address—training, staffing, and expertise—to help any agency protect their community from crime emanating from the dark web. The following recommendations set a good foundation to respond to the growing trend of dark web–related crimes.

Training

The veil of obscurity must be lifted to bring law enforcement agencies into the 21st century. Line officers and detectives must learn to recognize and deal with crimes on the dark web.[25] Internal and external training is pivotal in this regard. Although each agency is different in size and budget, every officer should understand the basic elements of the dark web. Line officers must know how to recognize criminals or crimes that may have a nexus to the dark web. Detectives must learn the basics so that they can call in experts when necessary and properly document any nexus to the dark web on reports. Managers and executives must become aware of the dark web to ensure their officers and detectives are properly identifying any connection crimes might have to it.

Although resources exist online, such as the IACP Cyber Center website and the National White Collar Criminal Center, little specific training on the dark web exists.[26] Much of these resources are focused on overall cybercrime-related material such as malware and cyber bullying. Further, these resources are generally focused on the seasoned detective. Therefore police academies should include basic dark web training to ensure that new officers have general knowledge about the topic. Further, patrol officer training should be developed to both expose officers to the key elements and to highlight detection strategies for dark web–related crimes. As an example, all officers should know that a ".onion" web address or locating a cryptocurrency wallet might indicate a dark web nexus. The more advanced courses should be reserved for detectives and civilian cybersecurity specialists. Recruit and in-service training, though, should keep pace with the changing nature of crime so reports from the field reach specialists with the needed initial information.

Staffing

Criminals operate on the dark web everywhere—the key is to identify those crimes and actors that overlap with local jurisdictions. The more agencies working on the dark web, the better the interagency collaboration and the more borderless each agency becomes, as shown by interagency success such as those by the INTERPOL Cybercrime Expert Group. The US Department of Justice, Federal Bureau of Investigation, and many large agencies have specialists that understand the dark web; however, many agencies do not participate in cyber task forces.

Depending upon the size of an agency and geographic restrictions, a detective or detectives that understand the realities of the dark web should be developed and maintained. Further, dark web detectives should participate in external multiagency task forces, even if only in an adjunct role. If the jurisdiction does not have a task force available or developed, local chiefs and sheriffs should consider creating a task force within a specific region or state. Large agencies that currently have established dark web specialists should analyze existing staffing levels and make appropriate considerations to increase staffing and expand involvement in the dark web.

However, peace officers should not be expected to be technical experts in the field of cybercrimes and the dark web.[27] Although officers should be aware of the elements of the crime and have general knowledge of the dark web, peace officers should maintain the key roles of law enforcement—identifying criminal activity, documenting crimes, seeking and executing search warrants, and making arrests. Experts in technical data security and dark web crimes should be the first line of expertise; sworn personnel should supplement their efforts and serve as the enforcement arm.

Experts

Due to the transient nature of detectives through rotations, transfers, or promotions, it is unrealistic to expect sworn officers to become information technology experts and long-term assets to dark web investigations. This concept is well known when it comes to the field of forensics and crime analysis—in many jurisdictions, crime scene specialists and crime analysts are civilian specialists with advanced degrees and training. These civilians have scientific and data analysis backgrounds and excel in what they do, and they tend to remain in their roles for longer periods of time. They are the behind-the-scenes experts that support and allow law enforcement to ultimately solve the crime and conduct an arrest.[28]

An example of a successful program can be found with the Federal Bureau of Investigation's Computer Scientist job classification. This classification, requiring a bachelor's degree in computer science and advanced mathematics, is a civilian position that assists federal agents investigating cybercrimes and investigations.[29] Similar job classifications and missions exist at the National Security Agency, although their missions involve national security instead of criminal investigations. Computer scientists are significantly different than the more common information technology classification, which handles computer troubleshooting.

There are challenges with creating a computer scientist investigator classification. The Federal Bureau of Investigation reports an overall shortage of computer scientists on staff and difficulty hiring them. Although there is considerable interest, due to basic hiring standards, the number of qualified applicants is limited.[30] Further, the National Security Agency reports losing an average of up to 25 percent of their existing computer scientists on staff, noting that outgoing employees enjoy the work and mission, but are driven away by the low salary.[31] Other challenges exist when an agency is trying to fill positions that require significant technical expertise. Contractors have been retained for that purpose, but agencies should consider their qualifications and backgrounds carefully to avoid possible breaches of trust or other misconduct, such as the story of Edward Snowden, a contractor who leaked classified information to the public.

Fortunately, law enforcement executives are no strangers to hiring challenges. The sheer number of computer scientist applicants to the Federal Bureau of Investigation shows an interest in this job track. Agencies can examine their own hiring practices to determine requirements for the position. Further, although law enforcement cannot compete with private sector job salaries in this regard, law enforcement must highlight the mission—law enforcement can offer the deep satisfaction of being involved with combating cyber criminals and assisting with making arrests and convictions. Job satisfaction is one of the primary drivers for computer science employees.[32]

Unfortunately, computer scientists supplementing sworn law enforcement is not widely used outside of federal agencies. Law enforcement executives must realize the importance of having computer scientists on staff and utilize them when it comes to dark web criminal investigations. Cybersecurity is a highly specialized field with highly compensated and educated employees. A civilian law enforcement computer scientist investigator position would support sworn detectives, while ensuring knowledge transfer and retention.

Conclusion

To help prevent and investigate dark web–associated crimes, law enforcement executives must recognize this emerging problem and then seek proper budgeting, ensure their departments are adequately trained, and ensure their detectives are supplemented by computer scientists. By developing and implementing these recommendations, local agencies will be structured to combat the problems of the dark web impacting their communities. As local agencies begin to focus their response and local leaders see the need for funding and supporting this effort, the network of law enforcement monitoring of the dark web will grow. Agencies, working together, will be able to send a strong message that the dark web is not as anonymous as criminals might be led to believe.

The dark web is a highly complex and technical platform that allows criminals to collaborate and sell the fruits of their crimes. Law enforcement also has a responsibility to become actively engaged to prevent and investigate all crimes—even those involving the dark web. Through basic awareness, as well as proper funding, training, and hiring practices, law enforcement agencies will be poised to reduce dark web–enabled crime. It should be the goal of every executive to ensure the dark web is no longer a safe haven for crime, guarding yet another alleyway through which the public can safely travel.

Notes

1. Thomas L. Friedman, *The World Is Flat* (New York, NY: Picador/Farrar, Straus and Giroux, 2007).

2. Internet Live Stats, "Internet Users."

3. Tim Berners-Lee, "The WorldWide Web Browser."

4. Internet Live Stats, "Internet Users."

5. Michelle F. Wright, "The Relationship Between Young Adults' Beliefs About Anonymity and Subsequent Cyber Aggression," *CyberPsychology, Behavior & Social Networking* 16, no. 12 (December 2013): 858–862.

6. Cadie Thompson, "Beyond Google: Everything You Need to Know About the Hidden Internet," *Business Insider*, December 16, 2015.

7. Thompson, "Beyond Google."

8. Thompson, "Beyond Google."

9. Corianna Jacoby, "The Onion Router and the Darkweb," December 15, 2016.

10. Andy Greenberg, "The Silk Road Creator's Life Sentence Actually Boosted Dark Web Drug Sales," *Wired*, May 23, 2017.

11. "5 Predictions for the Future of the Deep Web," *Buiness Reporter*, June 22, 2015.

12. Joseph Cox, "The Dark Web as You Know It Is a Myth," *Wired*, June 18, 2015.

13. Christopher Budd, "Why Is the Deep Web Eludcing Law Enforcement?" *TrendMicro Simply Security* (blog), August 5, 2016.

14. Paul Waldman, "Expert: U.S. Police Training in Use of Deadly Force Woefully Inadequate," *The American Prospect*, August 27, 2014.

15. Alexis Stevens, "Latest Crimes Show Dangers of Using Craigslist or Similar Websites," *Atlanta Journal-Consititution*, May 25, 2017.

16. Gabriella Paiella, "The U.S. Government Seized Backpage.com and Shut It Down," *The Cut* (blog), April 6, 2018.

17. Ahmed Ghappour, "Searching Places Unknown: Law Enforcement Jurisdiction on the Dark Web," *Stanford Law Review* 69, no. 4 (April 2017), 1075–1136.

18. Jacoby, "The Onion Router and the Darkweb."

19. Jonathan Mayer, "Cybercrime Litigation," *University of Pennsylvania Law Review* 164, no. 6 (2016): 1453–1507.

20. George Kelling and James Wilson, "Broken Windows: The Police and Neighborhood Safety," *Atlantic* (March 1982).

21. Internet Live Stats, "Internet Users."

22. Tom Spring, "Tor Developer Busts Myths, Announces New Features," ThreatPost, August 4, 2017 ; Sion Wyn Irfon Davies, *An Investigion into Whether 18–30 Year Olds View the Dark Web as Relevant—A Perspective of Cyber Privacy* (dissertation, Cardiff Metropolitan University, April 2017).

23. Spring, "Tor Developer Busts Myths."

24. Budd, "Why Is the Deep Web Eluding Law Enforcement?"

25. Budd, "Why Is the Deep Web Eluding Law Enforcement?"

26. IACP, Law Enforcement Cyber Center.

27. Erin Murphy, "The Mismatch Between Twenty-First-Century Forensic Evidence and Our Antiquated Criminal Justice System," *Southern California Law Review* 87 (2013–2014): 633–672.

28. Benjamin Mueller, "Police Add Civilians in Bid to Better Analyze Crime Data," *New York Times*, August 15, 2017.

29. Federal Bureau of Investigation "FBI Jobs: STEM."

30. Jack Moore, "Computer Scientists in Short Supply at FBI, Watchdog Warns," Nextgov, November 16, 2015.

31. Jack Moore, "In Fierce Battle for Cyber Talent, Even NSA Struggles to Keep Elites on Staff," Nextgov, April 14, 2015.

32. Kamlesh Mehta and Ronald Uhlig, "Business Administration and Computer Science Degrees: Earnings, Job Security, And Job Satisfaction," *American Journal of Business Education* 10, no. 1 (2017).

With International Cooperation, Law Enforcement Can Effectively Monitor the Dark Web

Europol

Europol is the European Union's law enforcement agency. It is headquartered in The Hague and aims to support a safer European Union for all citizens.

Months of preparation and coordination have resulted today, 20 July 2017, in the takedown of two of the largest criminal Dark Web markets, AlphaBay and Hansa.

Two major law enforcement operations, led by the Federal Bureau of Investigation (FBI), the US Drug Enforcement Agency (DEA) and the Dutch National Police, with the support of Europol, have shut down the infrastructure of an underground criminal economy responsible for the trading of over 350,000 illicit commodities including drugs, firearms and cybercrime malware. The coordinated law enforcement action in Europe and the US ranks as one of the most sophisticated takedown operations ever seen in the fight against criminal activities online.

"This is an outstanding success by authorities in Europe and the US," Rob Wainwright, the Executive Director of Europol, said today, while appearing alongside the US Attorney General, Acting FBI Director and Deputy Director of the US Drug Enforcement Administration (DEA), at a special press conference in Washington DC. "The capability of drug traffickers and other serious criminals around the world has taken a serious hit today after a highly sophisticated joint action in multiple countries. By acting together on a global basis the law enforcement community has sent a clear message that we have the means to identify criminality and strike

"Massive Blow to Criminal Dark Web Activities after Globally Coordinated Operation," European Union Agency for Law Enforcement Cooperation, July 20, 2017. Reprinted by permission.

back, even in areas of the Dark Web. There are more of these operations to come," he added.

Dimitris Avramopoulos, European Commissioner for Migration, Home Affairs and Citizenship, said: "The Dark Web is growing into a haven of rampant criminality. This is a threat to our societies and our economies that we can only face together, on a global scale. The take-down of the two largest criminal Dark Web markets in the world by European and American law enforcement authorities shows the important and necessary result of international cooperation to fight this criminality. I congratulate the American and Dutch authorities for their successful work, as well as Europol for centrally supporting this endeavour. Our fight against criminal activities online and offline will continue and intensify."

Julian King, EU Commissioner for the Security Union, said: "This latest success demonstrates not just the growing threat posed by increasingly sophisticated criminal enterprises exploiting the largely unregulated space occupied by the internet but also the vital role of international cooperation among law enforcers, the private sector, national authorities and international organisations in making all of us safer from global, borderless menaces."

Popular Dark Web Marketplaces

AlphaBay was the largest criminal marketplace on the Dark Web, utilising a hidden service on the Tor network to effectively mask user identities and server locations. Prior to its takedown, AlphaBay reached over 200,000 users and 40,000 vendors. There were over 250,000 listings for illegal drugs and toxic chemicals on AlphaBay, and over 100,000 listings for stolen and fraudulent identification documents and access devices, counterfeit goods, malware and other computer hacking tools, firearms, and fraudulent services. A conservative estimation of USD 1 billion was transacted in the market since its creation in 2014. Transactions were paid in Bitcoin and other cryptocurrencies. Hansa was the third largest criminal marketplace on the Dark Web, trading similarly high volumes in illicit drugs and other commodities. The two markets were created to facilitate the expansion of a major underground criminal economy, which affected the lives of thousands of people around the world and was expressly designed to frustrate the ability of law enforcement to bring offenders to justice.

The Investigations

Europol has been supporting the investigation of criminal marketplaces on the Dark Web for a number of years. With the help of Bitdefender, an internet security company advising Europol's European Cybercrime Centre (EC3), Europol provided Dutch authorities with an investigation lead into Hansa in 2016. Subsequent enquiries located the Hansa market infrastructure in the Netherlands, with follow-up investigations by the Dutch police leading to the arrest of its two administrators in Germany and the seizure of servers in the Netherlands, Germany and Lithuania. Europol and partner agencies in those countries supported the Dutch National Police to take over the Hansa marketplace on 20 June 2017 under Dutch judicial authorisation, facilitating the covert monitoring of criminal activities on the platform until it was shut down today, 20 July 2017. In the past few weeks, the Dutch Police collected valuable information on high value targets and delivery addresses for a large number of orders. Some 10 000 foreign addresses of Hansa market buyers were passed on to Europol.

In the meantime, an FBI and DEA-led operation, called Bayonet, was able to identify the creator and administrator of AlphaBay, a Canadian citizen living a luxurious life in Thailand. On 5 July 2017, the main suspect was arrested in Thailand and the site taken down. Millions of dollars worth of cryptocurrencies were frozen and seized. Servers were also seized in Canada and the Netherlands.

Law Enforcement Strategy

In shutting down two of the three largest criminal marketplaces on the Dark Web, a major element of the infrastructure of the underground criminal economy has been taken offline. It has severely disrupted criminal enterprises around the world, has led to the arrest of key figures involved in online criminal activity, and yielded huge amounts of intelligence that will lead to further investigations. But what made this operation really special was the strategy developed by the FBI, DEA, the Dutch Police and Europol to magnify the disruptive impact of the joint action to take out AlphaBay and Hansa. This involved taking covert control of Hansa under Dutch judicial authority a month ago, which allowed Dutch police to monitor the activity of users without their knowledge, and then shutting down AlphaBay during the same period. It meant the Dutch police could identify and disrupt the regular criminal activity on Hansa but then also sweep up all those new users displaced from AlphaBay who were looking for a new trading platform. In fact they flocked to Hansa in their droves, with an eight-fold increase in the number of new members of Hansa recorded immediately following the shutdown of AlphaBay. As a law enforcement strategy, leveraging the combined operational and technical strengths of multiple agencies in the US and Europe, it has been an extraordinary success and a stark illustration of the collective power the global law enforcement community can bring to disrupt major criminal activity.

Europol as a Central Hub

Europol has played a coordinating and de-conflicting role in both investigations. From the outset, Europol's European Cybercrime Centre (EC3) provided technical and forensic support to the Hansa marketplace investigation. In addition Europol's technical expertise was made available to the Dutch investigators in clouding on-the-spot deployment, as they gained control of Hansa. Subsequently to this, intelligence packages were prepared and sent out to law enforcement partners across 37 countries, spawning many follow-up investigations across Europe and beyond. Some of the intelligence extracted contains relevant information regarding the destination of drugs and is meant to inform the relevant countries about planned shipments of drugs. Overall more than 38,000 transactions have been identified and Europol sent more than 600 communications. To ensure smooth coordination between the two investigations into AlphaBay and Hansa, Europol hosted a coordination meeting with leading law enforcement partners. Overall, 12 different agencies sat down together and collectively mapped out and agreed the overall strategy for the two operations.

In early July, Europol hosted a command post staffed with representatives from the US FBI, DEA and Department of Justice, working alongside specialist staff from EC3. This command post was the central hub for information exchange during the AlphaBay operation. Europol's secure communication channels were used to exchange information between and receive data contributions from partners. Europol continues to support the FBI, DEA, the Dutch National Police and other partners on the forensic work that needs to be performed on huge amounts of seized material.

Tools for Monitoring the Dark Web Show Inconsistent Results

SpyCloud

SpyCloud is an information security company that helps businesses prevent and recover from data breaches and other security threats.

By now we've all heard of the dark web, but it's often misunderstood. One of the best ways to visualize the internet is as an iceberg The exposed portion we can see is literally only the tip. This is where the search engines and public websites can be found. We are comfortable with this "Surface Web" as it is where most of us spend the majority of our time.

What lies beneath is less known, but can be nefarious the deeper you go. What's just under the surface is considered the "Deep Web." This level contains a vast store of information, websites and files that have not been indexed by search engines. It also contains more sensitive websites that require the user to authenticate themselves through a username and password, such as a university's resources. Company intranet sites, medical portals, subscription-based websites, government resources and other entities websites are located here.

The bottom-most level of the iceberg is what is referred to as the "Dark Web," which has become infamous for its seedy reputation as a hotbed of drugs, pornography, and a general haven for questionable transactions. From illegally-obtained data to human trafficking sites, the dark web is not for the faint of heart. It requires specific software to access and is the playground for many types of criminals.

Why Is the Dark Web So Scary?

The dark web is not-so-secret, but it does contain plenty of information that is hidden from the majority of the population.

"Do Dark Web Monitoring Tools Work?" SpyCloud, Inc. Reprinted by permission.

For the cybercriminal and those who seek to discover their communities, it is the preferred sliver of the iceberg.

Cybercriminals hide in the dark web, communicating with each other and selling their stolen goods while aiming to evade detection. In the case of a data breach, such as Yahoo and LinkedIn, massive amounts of stolen personal information are sold on the dark web. It's where usernames, passwords, social security and driver's license numbers, credit card numbers, bank account information and much more is bought and sold to the highest bidder. They typically use cryptocurrencies such as bitcoin, z-cash, and monero which were designed to be virtually untraceable.

Often, we what we fear most is the unknown. Because we, as the general public, do not have access to the dark web, we aren't certain of what's there. What's even scarier is that most of us realize that something about us is likely there, but we have no idea what it is or how it may be leveraged against us. In this case, money is power.

How Does Information Get into the Dark Web?

Stealing personal information is a cybercriminal's full-time job. Some criminals specializing in credential theft can bring in as much as $2 million per year. They use sophisticated technologies, such as specific software and bots, to crack passwords. They break through company firewalls and infiltrate even the largest companies. Data breaches have become so common, we often ignore the warnings to change passwords.

This brings us to another issue. Passwords are meant to provide unique access to sensitive websites and information. Unfortunately, most people choose weak passwords—those that are too short, too simple and too easily guessed. To make things worse, people use the same password (or a slightly modified version) across multiple accounts. As soon as one account is breached, criminals can use those stolen credentials to break into all of the other accounts that use the same password. This can happen regularly and at scale in within seconds.

Once criminals breach a company's system, they take ownership over all of their newfound data. They either use that data to take over user accounts in order to steal money or they advertise their bounty on the dark web in an attempt to get other cybercriminals to purchase the data. Often, they do both.

Which Dark Web Monitoring Tools Are Used and Do They Work?

The only way to catch the thieves and discover stolen credentials is to invest in a dark web monitoring tool. Consumers and organizations hoping to protect their employees and customers (and thus their sensitive data) cannot monitor the dark web on their own. They must hire a dark web monitoring service that has the right technology and techniques to do it for them.

Scanners, Crawlers and Scrapers

Dark web monitoring most commonly involves scanners, crawlers and scrapers that spend time in dark web forums where the stolen credentials are being advertised and sold. Once they pick up a match, they alert the account owner or company that their credentials have been compromised.

Unfortunately, scanners, crawlers and scrapers find stolen credentials too late for the victim to do much about it. By the time the stolen credentials are discovered on dark web forums, they have been used, abused and sold multiple times. The key is to find exposures as soon as they happen before criminals have time to do anything with them.

Password Resets, Notifications and Multi-Factor Authentication

Once exposed credentials are discovered, some dark web monitoring tools automatically force the victim to change their password to an uncompromised one before they can log back into the system. Others simply notify the user their credentials were discovered in the dark web and prompt them to change their passwords. Sometimes they require a second authentication factor to verify the user is actually who they say they are and not a cybercriminal who has taken over the account.

While these extra steps do help with authentication, they are only enacted after the fact. None of the aforementioned dark web monitoring efforts do much to actually prevent stolen credentials from being used to take over an account.

Tools that Find Exposed Credentials Before ATO Can Happen
The only way to stop account takeover is to catch the exposure as soon as it happens. Not many tools have this capability. It requires the dark web monitoring service to use technology that is as sophisticated or more so than what the criminals use. Human intelligence can be used to establish covert relationships with cybercriminals. This strategy provides a one-two punch, digging deeper into the dark web, well-beyond forums and uncovering data breaches within hours of the breach.

The best dark web monitoring tool will do more than simply find exposed data. It will cleanse the data and crack hashed passwords so that victimized companies and organizations can actually use the data. It will empower victims with context around the exposure so the frequency and severity of the exposure are understood in order to direct the appropriate remediation techniques.

Not all dark web monitoring tools work. Some don't go far enough, others are too late, and many don't operationalize the data they uncover. Find one that goes deeper, discovers exposures earlier and makes the data usable. It's the only way to prevent account takeover and give you the return on your investment you expect.

Dark Web Monitoring Services Carry Risks of Their Own

Troy Hunt

Troy Hunt is a regional director for Microsoft in Australia. He also designs courses for Pluralsight and consults on a variety of information and data security projects including Have I Been Pwned (HIBP), a free service that aggregates data breaches and assists victims of malicious web activity.

No matter how much anyone tries to sugar coat it, a service like Have I been pwned (HIBP) which deals with billions of records hacked out of other peoples' systems is always going to sit in a grey area. There are degrees, of course; at one end of the spectrum you have the likes of Microsoft and Amazon using data breaches to better protect their customers' accounts. At the other end, there's services like the now defunct LeakedSource who happily sold our personal data (including mine) to anyone willing to pay a few bucks for it.

As far as intent goes, HIBP sits at the white end of the scale, as far to that extreme as I can possibly position it. It's one of many things I do in the security space alongside online training, conference talks, in-person workshops and of course writing this blog. All of these activities focus on how we can make security on the web better; increasing awareness, reducing the likelihood of a successful attack and minimising the damage if it happens. HIBP was always intended to amplify those efforts and indeed it has helped me do that enormously.

What I want to talk about here today is why I've made many of the decisions I have regarding the implementation of HIBP. This post hasn't been prompted by any single event, rather it seeks to address questions I regularly see coming up. I want to explain my thinking, explore why I've made many of the decisions I have and invite people to contribute comments with a hope of making it a more useful system for everyone.

The Accessibility of a Publicly Searchable System

The foremost question that comes up as it relates to privacy is "why make the system publicly searchable?" There are both human and technical reasons for this and I want to start with the former.

Returning an immediate answer to someone who literally asks the question "have I been pwned?" is enormously powerful. The immediacy of the response addresses a question that's clearly important to them at that very moment and from a user experience perspective, you simply cannot beat it.

The value in the UX of this model has significantly contributed to the growth of the service and as such, the awareness its raised. A great example is when you see someone take another person through the experience: "here, you just enter your email address and... whoa!" The penny suddenly drops that data breaches are a serious thing and thus begins the discussion about password strength and reuse, multi-step verification and other fundamental account management hygiene issues.

The fact that someone can search for someone who is not them is a double-edged sword; the privacy risk is obvious in that you may discover someone was in a particular data breach and then use that information to somehow disadvantage them. However, people also extensively use the service to help protect other people, for example by identifying exposed spouses, friends, relatives or even customers and advising them accordingly.

I heard a perfect example of this just the other day when speaking to a security bod in a bank. He explained how HIBP was used when communicating with customers who'd suffered an account takeover. By highlighting that they'd appeared in a breach such as LinkedIn, they are able to help the customer understand the potential source of the compromise. Without being able to publicly locate that customer in HIBP, it would be a much less feasible proposition for the bank.

I mitigate the risk of public discoverability adversely impacting someone by flagging certain breaches as "sensitive" and excluding them from publicly visible results. This concept came in when the Ashley Madison data hit and the only way to see if you're in that data breach (or any other that poses a higher risk of disadvantaging someone) is to receive an email to the searched address and click on a unique link (I'll come back to why I don't do that for all searches in a moment).

I've actually had many people suggest that it's ok to show the sensitive results I'm presently returning privately because the privacy of these individuals has already been compromised due to the original breach. I don't like this argument and the main reason is because I don't believe the act of someone else having illegally broken into another system means the victims of that breach should be exposed further in ways that would likely disadvantage them. It's not the only time I've heard this, for example after launching Pwned Passwords last month a number of people said "you should just return email address and password pairs because their data is out there anyway." Shortly after that, I was told I'm "holding people hostage" by not providing the passwords for compromised email addresses. In fact, I had someone get quite irate about that after loading the Onliner Spambot data with the bloke in question then proceeding to claim that not disclosing it wasn't protecting anyone. Someone else suggested I was "too old fashioned and diplomatic." No! These all present a significantly greater risk for those individuals and for someone who himself is in HIBP a dozen times now, I'd be pretty upset if I saw any of this happening.

Searching by Email Verification Is Fraught with Problems

This is the alternative I most frequently hear—"just email the results." There are many reasons why this is problematic and I've already touched on the first above: the UX is terrible. There's no immediate response and instead you're stuck waiting for an email to arrive. Now you may argue that a short wait is worth the trade-off, but there's much more to it than that.

HIBP gets shared and used constructively in all sorts of environments that depend on an immediate response. For example, it gets a huge amount of press and a search is regularly shown in news pieces. Many people (particularly in the infosec community) use it at conference talks and they're not about to go opening up their personal email to show a result.

But those are arguments in favour of accessibility and I appreciate not everyone will agree with them so let's move onto hard technical challenges and the first is delivering email. It's very hard. In all honesty, the single most difficult (and sometimes the single most expensive) part of running this service is delivering mail and doing it reliably. Let's start there actually—here's the cost of sending 700k emails via SendGrid: $399.95/mo.

Now fortunately, SendGrid helps support the project so I don't end up wearing that cost but you can see the problem. Let's just put the challenge of sending an email on every search in context for a moment: a few weeks ago, I had 2.8 million unique visitors in just one day after making the aforementioned 711 million record Onliner Spambot dump searchable. Each one of those people did *at least* one search and if I was to pay for that volume, here's what I'd be looking at: $1,174.95/mo.

That's one day of traffic. I can't run a free service that way and I hate to think of the discussion I'd be having with my wife if I did! Now that was one *exceptional* day but even in low periods I'm still talking about many millions of visitors a month. As it is, I'm coming very close to maxing out my email allocation each month just from sending verification emails and notifications when I load breaches. And no, a cheaper service like Amazon SES is not a viable alternative, I've been down that path before and it was a debacle for many reasons plus would still get very pricey. (Incidentally, large volumes of emails in a spike often causes delivery to be throttled which would further compound the UX problem of people waiting for a search result to land.)

And then there's the deliverability problems. One of the single hardest challenges I have is reliably getting mail through to people's inbox.

DKIM is good. SPF is good. I have a dedicated IP. I'm not on any black lists. Everything checks out fine yet consistently, I hear people say "your notification went to junk." I suspect it's due to the abnormal sending patterns of HIBP, namely that when I load a breach there's a sudden massive spike of emails sent but even then, it's only ever to HIBP subscribers who've successfully double-opted-in. So, think of what that would mean in terms of using email as the sole channel for sharing breach exposure: a heap of people are simply going to miss out. They won't know they were exposed in a breach, they won't adapt their behaviour and for them, HIBP becomes useless.

I've seen criticism from other services attempting to do similar things to HIBP based on the fact I'm not just sending emails to answer that "have I been pwned?" question. But they're at a very different stage of maturity and popularity and simply don't have these challenges—it's be a lot easier if I was only sending hundreds of emails a day and not tens or sometimes even hundreds of thousands. They're also often well-funded and commercialise their visitors so you can see why they may not understand the unique challenges I face with HIBP.

In short, this is the best possible middle ground I can find. Not everyone agrees with it, but I hope that even the folks who don't can see it's a reasoned, well thought out conclusion.

Because I Don't Want Your Email Address

There are a number of different services out there which offer the ability to identify various places your data has been spread across the web. It's a similar deal to HIBP insofar as you enter an email address to begin the search, but many then promise to "get back to you" with results. Of course, during this time, they retain your address. How long do they retain it for? Well...

Someone directed me to Experian's "Dark Web Email Scan" service just recently. I had the feeling just from reading the front page that there was more going on than meets the eye so I took a look at the policies they link to and that (in theory) you must read and agree to before proceeding.

Folks who've *actually read all this* have subsequently pointed out that as expected, providing your address in this way now opts you into all sorts of things you really don't want. In fact, I saw it myself first hand.

In other words, the service is a marketing funnel. The premise of "just leave us with your address and we'll get back to you" is often a thin disguise to build up a list of potential customers. Part of the beauty of HIBP returning results immediately is that the searched address never goes into a database. The only time this happens is when the user explicitly opts in to the notification service in which case I obviously need the address in order to contact them later should they appear in a new data breach. It's data minimisation to the fullest extent I can; I don't want anything I don't absolutely, positively need.

Incidentally, by Experian not explicitly identifying the site the breach occurred on it makes it *extremely* difficult for people to actually action the report. They're not the only ones—I've seen other services do this too—and it leaves the user thinking "what the hell do I do now?!" I know this because it's precisely the feedback I had after loading the Onliner Spambot data I mentioned earlier, the difference being that I simply didn't know with any degree of confidence where that data originated from. But when I do, I tell people—it's just the right thing to do.

The API Is an Important Part of the Ecosystem

One of the best things I did very early on in terms of making the service accessible to a broad range of people was to publish an

API. In additional to that, I list a number of the consumers of the service and they've done some great things done with it. There are many other very good use cases you won't see publicly listed and that I can't talk about here, but you can imagine the types of positive implementations ingenious people have come up with.

In many cases, the API has enabled people to do great things for awareness.

The very nature of having an API that can search breaches in the fashion means the data has to be publicly searchable. Even if I put API keys on the thing, I'd then have the challenge of working out who I can issue them to then policing their use of the service. For all the reasons APIs make sense for other software projects, they make sense for HIBP.

Now, having said all that, the API has had to evolve over time. Last year I introduced a rate limit after seeing usage patterns that were not in keeping with ethical use of the service. As a result, one IP can now only make a request every 1.5 seconds and anything over that is blocked. Keep it up and the IP is presented with a JavaScript challenge at Cloudflare for 24 hours. Yes, you can still run a lot of searches but instead of 40k a minute as I was often seeing from a single IP, we're down to 40. In other words, the worst-case scenario is only one one-thousandth of what it previously was. What that's done is forced those seeking to abuse the system to seek the data out from other places as the effectiveness of using HIBP has plummeted.

Like many of the decisions I've made to protect individuals who end up in HIBP, this one has also garnered me criticism. Very often I feel like I'm damned if I do and I'm damned if I don't; some people were unhappy in this case because it made some of the things they used to do suddenly infeasible. Yes, it slashed malicious use but you can also see how it could impact legitimate use of the API too. I'm never going to be able to make everyone happy with these decisions, I just have to do my best and continue trying to strike the right balance.

I'm Still Adamant About Not Sharing Passwords Attached to Email Addresses

A perfect example of where I simply don't see eye to eye with some folks is sharing passwords attached to email addresses. I've maintained since day 1 that this poses many risks and indeed there are many logistical problems with actually doing this, not least of which is the increasing use of stronger hashing algorithms in the source data breaches.

Not everyone has the same tolerance to risk in this regard. I mentioned earlier how some especially shady services will provide your personal data to anyone else willing to pay; passwords, birth dates, sexualities—it's all up for grabs. Others will email either the full password or a masked portion of it, both of which significantly increase the risk to the owner of that password should that email be obtained by a nefarious party.

I've tried to tackle the gap between providing a full set of credentials and only the email address by launching the Pwned Passwords service last month. Whilst the primary motivation here was to provide organisations with a means of identifying at-risk passwords during signup, it also helps individuals directly impacted by data breaches; find both your email address and a password you've used before on HIBP and that's a pretty solid sign you want to revisit your account management hygiene.

At the end of the day, no matter how well I was to implement a solution that attached email addresses to other classes of personal data, there's simply no arguing with the basic premise of I cannot lose what I do not have. I have to feel comfortable with the balance I strike in terms of how I handle this data and at present, that means not putting it online.

There Are Still a Lot of Personal Judgement Calls

I've been asked a few times now what the process for flagging a breach as sensitive is and the answer is simply this: I make a personal judgement call. I have to look at the nature of the service and question what the impact would be if HIBP was used as a vector to discover if someone has an account on that site. I don't always get this right.

HIBP is a constant series of judgement calls when it comes to the ethics of running the service. The data I should and should not load is another example. I didn't load the Australian Red Cross Blood Service breach because we managed to clean up all known copies of it (there are multiple reasons why I'm confident in that statement) and they committed to promptly notifying all impacted parties which they summarily did. I removed the VTech data breach because it gave parents peace of mind that data relating to kids was removed from all known locations. In both those cases, it was a judgement call made entirely of my own free volition; there were no threats of any kind, it was just the right thing to do.

HIBP is not about trying to maximise the data in the system, it's about helping people and organisations deal with serious criminal acts. Frankly, the best possible outcome would be for there to be no more breaches to load. This is what all my courses, workshops, conference talks and indeed hundreds of blog posts are trying to drive us towards—fixing the problems that have led to data breach search services being a thing in the first place. Not everyone has those same motives though, and that's leading us to some pretty shady practices.

The "No Shady Practices" Rule

As I said in the intro, there's no sugar-coating the fact that handling data breaches is always going to sit in a grey area. This makes it enormously important that every possible measure is taken to avoid any behaviour whatsoever that could be construed as shady. It probably shouldn't surprise anyone, but this is not a broadly held belief amongst those dealing with this class of data.

I mentioned LeakedSource earlier on; there are still multiple sites following the same business model of "give us a few bucks and we'll give you other people's data." There's a total disregard not just for the privacy of people like you and I, but for the impact it can then have on our lives. People bought access to my own data—I know this because someone once sent it to me! Many of these services operate with impunity under the assumption that they're anonymous; great lengths are gone to in order to obfuscate and shield the identity of the operators although as we saw with Leaked Source, anonymity can be fleeting.

There are also multiple organisations paying for data breaches. What this leads to is criminal incentivisation; rewarding someone for breaking into a system and pilfering the data in no way improves the very problem these services set out to address. Mind you, the argument could be made that the purpose these services primarily serve is to be profitable and viewed in that light, paying for data and then charging for access to it probably makes sense from an ROI perspective. I've never paid for data and I never intend to and yes, that means that it sometimes takes longer for it to appear on HIBP, but it's the right thing to do.

Ambulance chasing is another behaviour that's well and truly into the dark end of shady. I recently had a bunch of people contact me after an organisation emailed them to advise that addresses from their company were found in a breach. Then I watched just last month as someone representing another org hijacked Twitter threads mentioning HIBP in order to promote their own service (I then had to explain what was wrong with this practice, something I later highlighted in another thread). In all these cases, financial incentive either from directly monetising the service itself or indirectly promoting other services associated to the organisation appear to be the driver for shady practices.

We should all be beyond reproach when handling this data.

Summary

Being completely honest, it would have to be less than one in one thousand pieces of feedback I get that are critical or even the least bit concerned about the HIBP model as it stands today. It's a very rare thing and that may make you wonder why I even bothered writing this in the first place, but the truth is that it helped me get a few things straight in my own head whilst also providing a reference point for those who *do* express genuine concern.

HIBP remains a service that first and foremost serves to further ethical objectives. This primarily means raising awareness of the impact data breaches are having and helping those of us that have been stung by them to recover from the event. Even as I've built out commercial services for organisations that have requested them, you won't find a single reference to this on this site; there's no "products" or "pricing," no up-sell, no financial model for consumers, no withholding of information in an attempt to commercialise it, no shitty terms and conditions that you have to read before searching and not even any advertising or sponsorship. All of this is simply because I don't want *anything* detracting from that original objective I set forth.

I'll close this post out by saying that there will almost certainly be changes to this in the future. Indeed, it's constantly changed already; sensitive breaches, rate limits and the removal of the pastes listing are all examples of where I've stepped back, looked at the system and thought "this needs to be done better."

When It Comes to Dark Web Security, There Are No Easy Answers

Robert Gehl

Robert Gehl is a professor in the department of communication at the University of Utah. His research focuses on communication technology, new media theory, network cultures, and the political economy of communication systems.

In the wake of recent violent events in the US, many people are expressing concern about the tone and content of online communications, including talk of the "dark web." Despite the sinister-sounding phrase, there is not just one "dark web." The term is actually fairly technical in origin, and is often used to describe some of the lesser-known corners of the internet. As I discuss in my new book, "Weaving the Dark Web: Legitimacy on Freenet, Tor, and I2P," the online services that make up what has become called the "dark web" have been evolving since the early days of the commercial internet—but because of their technological differences, are not well understood by the public, policymakers or the media.

As a result, people often think of the dark web as a place where people sell drugs or exchange stolen information—or as some rare section of the internet Google can't crawl. It's both, and neither, and much more.

Seeking Anonymity and Privacy

In brief, dark websites are just like any other website, containing whatever information its owners want to provide, and built with standard web technologies, like hosting software, HTML and JavaScript. Dark websites can be viewed by a standard web

"Illuminating the 'Dark Web,'" by Robert Gehl, The Conversation, October 30, 2018. https://theconversation.com/illuminating-the-dark-web-105542. Licensed under CC BY 4.0 International.

browser like Firefox or Chrome. The difference is that they can only be accessed through special network-routing software, which is designed to provide anonymity for both visitors to websites and publishers of these sites.

Websites on the dark web don't end in ".com" or ".org" or other more common web address endings; they more often include long strings of letters and numbers, ending in ".onion" or ".i2p." Those are signals that tell software like Freenet, I2P or Tor how to find dark websites while keeping users' and hosts' identities private.

Those programs got their start a couple of decades ago. In 1999, Irish computer scientist Ian Clarke started Freenet as a peer-to-peer system for computers to distribute various types of data in a decentralized manner rather than through the more centralized structure of the mainstream internet. The structure of Freenet separates the identity of the creator of a file from its content, which made it attractive for people who wanted to host anonymous websites.

Not long after Freenet began, the Tor Project and the Invisible Internet Project developed their own distinct methods for anonymously hosting websites.

Today, the more commonly used internet has billions of websites—but the dark web is tiny, with tens of thousands of sites at the most, at least according to the various indexes and search engines that crawl these three networks.

A More Private Web

The most commonly used of the three anonymous systems is Tor—which is so prominent that mainstream websites like Facebook, The New York Times and The Washington Post operate versions of their websites accessible on Tor's network. Obviously, those sites don't seek to keep their identities secret, but they have piggybacked on Tor's anonymizing web technology in order to allow users to connect privately and securely without governments knowing.

In addition, Tor's system is set up to allow users to anonymously browse not only dark websites, but also regular websites. Using

Tor to access the regular internet privately is much more common than using it to browse the dark web.

Moral Aspects of "Dark" Browsing

Given the often sensationalized media coverage of the dark web, it's understandable that people think the term "dark" is a moral judgment. Hitmen for hire, terrorist propaganda, child trafficking and exploitation, guns, drugs and stolen information markets do sound pretty dark.

Yet people commit crimes throughout the internet with some regularity—including trying to hire killers on Craigslist and using Venmo to pay for drug purchases. One of the activities often associated with the dark web, terrorist propaganda, is far more prevalent on the regular web.

Defining the dark web only by the bad things that happen there ignores the innovative search engines and privacy-conscious social networking—as well as important blogging by political dissidents.

Even complaining that dark web information isn't indexed by search engines misses the crucial reality that search engines never see huge swaths of the regular internet either—such as email traffic, online gaming activity, streaming video services, documents shared within corporations or on data-sharing services like Dropbox, academic and news articles behind paywalls, interactive databases and even posts on social media sites. Ultimately, though, the dark web is indeed searchable as I explain in a chapter of my book.

Thus, as I suggest, a more accurate connotation of "dark" in "dark web" is found in the phrase "going dark"—moving communications out of clear and public channels and into encrypted or more private ones.

Managing Anxieties

Focusing all this fear and moral judgment on the dark web risks both needlessly scaring people about online safety and erroneously reassuring them about online safety.

For instance, the financial services company Experian sells services that purport to "monitor the dark web" to alert customers when their personal data has been compromised by hackers and offered for sale online. Yet to sign up for that service, customers have to give the company all sorts of personal information—including their Social Security number and email address—the very data they're seeking to protect. And they have to hope that Experian doesn't get hacked, as its competitor Equifax was, compromising the personal data of nearly every adult in the US.

It's inaccurate to assume that online crime is based on the dark web—or that the only activity on the dark web is dangerous and illegal. It's also inaccurate to see the dark web as content beyond the reach of search engines. Acting on these incorrect assumptions would encourage governments and corporations to want to monitor and police online activity—and risk giving public support to privacy-invading efforts.

Current
CONTROVERSIES

CHAPTER 3

Are There Safe and Legitimate Uses for the Dark Web?

A Map of the Dark Web and Its Resources

The British Computer Society

The British Computer Society (BCS) is a professional organization dedicated to raising the standards of IT education, professionalism, ethics, and practice. BCS has over 68,000 members in 150 countries around the world.

A s you read on, we'll explore how the "dark web" works, how big it is (and it is huge) and how most of it is relatively benign, but has gained notoriety because of a few places where illegal goods and services are sold to anyone willing to pay the price—and to take the risk.

What Is the "Dark Web"?

Read the term dark web and most people's minds leap immediately to the stuff of lurid headlines. The media often portrays the dark web as a den of vice and iniquity—a place where you can buy guns and drugs as readily as soap in your supermarket. And sure, there is criminality on the dark web. But this isn't the whole story by any means.

The dark web also goes by another, much less dramatic name: the deep web. The deep web is probably a more correct term because it conveys the idea that the internet is like an iceberg.

A small amount of the iceberg (around four per cent in this case) is above the waterline, and this, for our purposes, is the "'normal web"—the parts you can see via a search engine, and that search engines can index.

However, a clear majority of our iceberg is below the waterline. These are the things which a search engine cannot see. Think of

"Demystifying the Dark Web," The British Computer Society (BCS), May 2017. Reprinted by permission. This material first appeared in BCS, The Chartered Institute for IT's membership magazine *ITNOW*.

the servers your email, instant messages, and other non-web page data travels through.

These repositories do, however, make up a part of the dark or deep web. Far from being frightening and dangerous though, these are generally very safe places. You should, however, be aware that your daily life frequently involves the dark web in some way.

A Route to the Dark Web

The dark web is generally considered to be a group of websites which exist on a special type of network that cannot be seen by the "normal web." They are powered by places like "The Onion Router (TOR)" (torproject.org), "I2P" (geti2p.net), and "Freenet"(freenetproject.org), all of which offer specialist pieces of software which allow you to access the websites on the dark web.

Once you have one of these pieces of software installed, you can potentially access any of the websites on the dark web which comply with your software's protocols. It is worth noting though— often the most nefarious and notorious dark web sites also require passwords and access is by invitation only.

How Does the Dark Web Work?

Each web address or website on the dark web represents a starting point, or node, which allows the connection to reach the server the website is actually stored on.

These starting points, or nodes, provide access to a network, connected in a way to protect the identity of the person or people who run the websites which make up the dark web. All of these connections are encrypted, and it is almost impossible to block access to these networks.

These connections and the encryption which makes them up, makes remaining anonymous very easy on these websites. Anonymity isn't, however, complete and absolute, it should be noted.

This high level of anonymity is, of course, why the dark web and its supported sites have become a haven for criminals. Almost all of the servers on the dark web are set not to store logs or any information which could possibly reveal who you are.

The ISP you are using to connect to the internet will be able to monitor your activity however. But because of the encryption used throughout the dark web, they will not know what you are doing or the content of the pages you are visiting.

All this encryption and the necessary routing does have one downside that becomes immediately obvious: surfing the dark web can be very slow. All that anonymity comes at a price.

What Can You Find on the Dark Web?

You can find a lot of different things on the dark web, however you can only access a very small percentage of them using the encrypted networks. It is worth noting that many criminals, hackers and undesirable people have made the dark web their home.

Again, because of the desire for anonymity, the dark web ecommerce sites tend not to take credit cards. These are eminently traceable. Rather Bitcoin—and other crypto-currencies—are taken. These, in themselves, are generally safe enough. The problem is, should you decide to go shopping on the dark web, you'll soon discover that laissez-faire is king on the black market.

You can find versions of websites such as Facebook, Wikileaks, Twitter, and many other popular websites, all of which are designed specifically within their "dark web" counterparts, to facilitate anonymous access.

A Rough Guide to the Dark Web

In addition to copies of popular websites, you will also come across:

- Forums: discussion forums are a way for criminals and other people alike to communicate and share information with each other. Many criminal conspiracies are no-doubt planned and carried out because of conversations which take place on the dark web forums.
- Software downloads and serial key sharing: downloading illegal software, and sharing serial keys is commonplace

throughout the dark web, allowing some people to gain access to thousands of pounds worth of software for nothing.

- Hackers: the dark web is a marketplace for hackers to buy and sell their services, as well as to talk. They communicate with people who want to buy their services, commonly via forums.
- Illegal items of all types: that marketplace extends to illegal items, with everything from hitmen to drugs to counterfeit currency being available to buy from many of the ever growing list of marketplaces available on the dark web.
- Whistle-blowing platforms: Many people use the dark web for good. The anonymous nature of the dark web allows those who want to report problems with their governments or companies to do it freely and expose corruption or fraud whenever it exists. Because this is all conducted anonymously, it is never traced back to the person who reported it; ideal for whistle-blowing.

An Overview of The Onion Routing (TOR)

Onion routing is a multi-layer encryption and communication technique. It works by using multiple layers, like an onion, hence its name, which allow each device it passes through to know the next device and the previous device, but not the origin device or the destination device.

Each device the packets of data pass through decrypt their layer of the onion, before passing it onto the next device in the sequence. The details for where the next device is are stored in the encrypted data the current device decrypts.

It knows where the packets of data have come from, and it knows to where it is sending those packets of data, but it does not know where the packets of data originated, or where they will ultimately end up. This is the basic principle of onion routing.

Typically, when you send data packets across the internet, or a network, a log is kept of where they go, how big they are, and where they end up.

Using the principles of onion routing, you can make it very much more difficult for people to know who you were communicating with, along with what you were saying.

This makes the packets of data you are sending almost completely impossible to trace without either the start or end of the network giving you more information about the packet than would normally happen, for example, when the end device tells you all of the information within the packet because it has been compromised using malware or a virus.

Crypto-Market Security Depends on the Right Technology

Netsparker Ltd.

Netsparker is a company that specializes in the development of web application security products. Its clients include top technology firms like Samsung, NASA, Microsoft, and Siemens.

[…]

The concept of time and the things that happen during its slow progression is utterly staggering. Did you know Cleopatra lived closer in time to the Moon landing than she did to the Great Pyramid of Giza being built in Cairo, Egypt? Here is another mind-blowing realization: The concept of currency trade for goods—cash, coin, crops, cattle, whatever people deem as valuable and worthy of trade—has existed for at least over twice as long as recorded history itself. It is estimated that recorded history began around 4,000 B.C., whereas currency in the form of bartering for goods has been around since at least 9,000 B.C., perhaps much longer.

For perhaps just as long, black markets have existed as well. While a market is an economic institution where tangible currency in some form is exchanged in trade for goods or services, a black market is similar, but involves either the currency exchange itself or the goods or services being traded being illegal. This is done typically to circumvent regulatory powers, avoid detection, or simply to obtain illicit or illegal goods.

With everything becoming more advanced and evolving into a digital format, the world now relies on the Internet and electronic currency to continue uninterrupted on its unfathomably rapid pace. Currency has seen its evolution from the bartering of grains and goats, to coins and promissory notes, to ones and zeros on a bustling stock exchange floor zooming by with millisecond trades. Black markets also participated in this evolution, and while some of the illicit goods have remain unchanged (such as drugs), many new ones have been borne of this evolution, such as software to take down websites and log peoples' keystrokes.

With the evolution of currency from commodity to fiat—that is, backed by tangible goods, like gold, to being valued solely by federated banking institutions, respectively—federation of currency itself has come under fire as an indefinably corruptible system. Through very recent advancements in technology and software, currency federation itself has started to become a thing of the past—a windfall digital black markets are more than happy to exploit.

Untraceable, Undetectable—Anonymous Currency

The great thing about cash is that aside from physical forensics (e.g. fingerprints, DNA, locality-specific trace elements, etc.), it is virtually untraceable. Barring any form of surveillance, it leaves no record of who spent it. You never see drug dealers on Breaking Bad use credit cards to buy illicit substances, because the transaction is traceable. Cash is king, as the saying goes, because unlike digitized transactions where everything can and will be logged, traced, and archived, cash grants that anonymity and a better guarantee of not getting caught. But cash is still physical.

Fast forward to today's era, and everything relies on digital currency instead of cash. Unlike some European countries, like Germany for instance, the United States and others rely heavily upon ethereal currency in the form of a 16-digit debit or credit card number in lieu of cash at every available opportunity. Governments like this because it grants explicit and traceable detail for an indefinite length of time; Black market merchants and customers despise it for those very same reasons. This has inspired the desire for an anonymous and decentralized currency. Many have been proposed, though almost all had floundered due to poor planning, implementation, or simply lack of widespread adoption. For the longest time, this was just a pipedream—until 2008 happened.

In 2008, an entity that went by the name of Satoshi Nakamoto (either a single person or team of people pretending to be one) released the Bitcoin payment system. Designed as a decentralized virtual cryptocurrency (a currency exchange of whole or fractional "Bitcoins" using cryptography to ensure the security and integrity of transactions), the system utilizes an anonymous public ledger of hashed addresses of both wallets and the Bitcoins they possess. New Bitcoins are "mined" and generated by doing complex computations spread across entire server farms, growing in complexity with each new Bitcoin (or BTC) generated. No names, addresses, or any information is known except for a historical record of what wallets have what Bitcoins (or slices of Bitcoins). The Bitcoin system itself also affords a level of peer-to-peer always-online security, being unable to succumb as easily to things like Distributed Denial of Service (DDoS) attacks—a fate PayPal experienced in 2010 when it chose to freeze Wikileaks' account. While this system affords quite an astoundingly high level of anonymity, it still has its risks of being traced to individual users.

[…]

How Digital Black Markets Began—A Brief History

When everything in the world started the shift from analog to digital—or rather, from non-networked and offline to networked and online—so, too, did the idea of a black market. Originally, the concept began on systems like Usenet newsgroups. In the early days of the Internet, the world wide web did not yet exist, so people lucky enough to afford a 2,400 baud modem—the typical modem most users could enjoy for nearly 20 years—had to make due with simpler methods: email, bulletin board systems (BBS), and Usenet. Bulletin boards had some of these users, like the MindVox BBS and others, but Usenet groups are really where the concept flourished. The Usenet groups were often more difficult to find, too, which was a major reason for their popularity in this particular realm. Depending on the host—who were nowhere near as ubiquitous as they have been over the past decade—sometimes the content was heavily policed, but not always. With the proper newsreader client and server information, users could eventually find their way to these various shady Usenet groups that usually trafficked in illegal pornography, questionably legal electronics or software, and other items one would reasonably assume from such nefarious places, to perform their transactions.

[…]

Why Take the Risk?

Whatever the risk involved, some users of the Internet felt that being told what they can and cannot possess, physical or digital, was akin to oppression. Telling someone they cannot do something is among the easiest ways to inspire them to do it. Human beings are fascinating creatures for a lot of reasons, in particular that for even as logical as we are, we still do some incredibly foolish or backwards things. For example, if you tell a human, "No, you cannot do that, it is not allowed," they will find any conceivable method to do that which they are forbidden to do, even if it is utterly pointless to do so. This is especially apparent in children, but just as much so in adults. Thus, the theory goes, if you tell humans they are not allowed to purchase particular objects, or own certain items in ways they feel they are entitled to, then Hell or high water they will find a way to do it. This is undoubtedly a core reason, if not the core reason behind black markets existing—that rebellious nature inherent to self-awareness—and it remains just as true today as it did in the Assyrian era when black market bazaars first started to exist. Perhaps it could be argued that digital black markets—maybe not all, but some—exist under the belief of free information, free knowledge, and freedom to do with your purchase as you see fit, corporate content makers' controlling wishes be damned.

It all sounds very Robin Hood, like some 21st century "copy from the rich corporations, and give downloads to the poor consumers online" idea, but it also takes a horrifying turn from righteous to indignant and sometimes even downright disgusting with the click of a mouse. Within the ranks of these hackers that felt ethical in their liberation of data, some existed that wanted to profit from burning others. More questionable digital content came into the trade, including malware and virus sales, purchasable vulnerability information and more. With both the copyright industry coming down on the DRM circumvention and copyright infringement groups, and government alphabet soups (FBI, DOJ, SEC, etc.) coming down on the virus trade, these groups began going further underground. They found that to minimize risk, they would need to utilize end-to-end anonymity software, thus fostering a new iteration of digital black markets on a network colloquially termed the "dark web."

Expanding Our Understanding of the Dark Web

Michelle Bovée

Michelle Bovée is a market intelligence manager at MAGNA Global and a writer whose work focuses on global advertising and media. She holds a master's degree in international relations from the London School of Economics.

This year's Davos forum covered a lot of ground on issues relating to the human implications of digital media, including the ways in which terrorist organizations like the Islamic State leverage social media and how governments interact with the challenges and opportunities provided by increasing connectivity. But one key facet of the digital age was largely absent from Davos: the dark web.

The 2013 bust of Silk Road mastermind Dread Pirate Roberts (aka Ross Ulbricht) was the first time many people heard the phrase "dark web," which typically refers to the hidden corner of the web where anonymous users solicit drugs, prostitutes, hit men, child pornography, illicit arms, and any other illegal substance and/or activity imaginable. The dark web has another side, though: the side that provides the anonymity and access necessary for activists, journalists, and others who need to stay secure when protesting authoritarian regimes, providing tips for law enforcement, or reporting in countries with strict censorship laws. The role that the dark web plays in everything from illegal trafficking to terrorist fundraising to subverting Internet censorship ought to be taken into account when discussing the ways in which the web intersects with human rights, international relations, and politics. The many facets of the dark web deserve a nuanced discussion on the global

"International Relations in the Dark," by Michelle Bovée, Charged Affairs, March 23, 2016. Reprinted by permission.

stage, and Davos would have been an excellent forum for such a discussion.

The dark web has been used by terrorist organizations to spread propaganda, secure financing, and procure supplies. Around the time of the Paris attacks, for example, ISIS was discovered to have migrated to this underground channel. This was surprising, given the organization's propensity for relying on highly visible social media networks like Facebook and Twitter to spread their message and recruit new members, but it is likely that they were pushed to move some of their activities underground following hacktivist attempts to hinder their operations. Of course, it's highly probable that ISIS members were already involved with the dark web, exploiting the anonymous nature of the marketplace to raise funds, traffic weapons, and distribute training manuals and avoid being tracked by international regulators.

Though ISIS's dark web use has been thrust into the spotlight, many people around the world benefit from the security and anonymity offered by Tor browser, the most commonly used software for dark web access. Journalists, government agents, dissidents, and activists all use the network to transmit crucial information about the conditions on the ground in locations that restrict access to information. It was widely used, for example, in Egypt's Arab Spring uprisings by activists looking to circumvent government censorship and access the social media sites used to plan demonstrations and spread information outside the country. Even average web users in non-oppressive countries are coming to rely on Tor to protect their privacy and casually browse the web without being tracked by advertisers.

Clearly, the dark web has uses beyond terrorist financing or trafficking. Indeed, it seems, at times, that the dark web is everywhere, intertwined with everything from international terrorism to global activist movements to ordinary, confidential web access. This means, for better or worse, policymakers and international organizations are going to have to figure out how to cope with this wild west of the Internet, how to trace and prevent illegal activity while preserving the secure elements used by reporters and activists alike. International organizations that focus on counterterrorism efforts, like INTERPOL (which has published a number of articles on the subject), could benefit from an open discussion with world leaders on the ways in which the hidey-hole of the dark web facilitates terrorist activity and how this can be remedied, while organizations aimed at protecting individual liberties on the web, like the Global Internet Freedom Consortium, could discuss novel ways to raise awareness of how to use Tor to provide secure, anonymous internet access.

A global, nuanced dialogue that acknowledges that the dark web is more than just a buying place for black-market goods or a channel for terrorist activity is the first step towards identifying ways to reduce illegal activity while maintaining the components that protect journalists and human rights activists. Any unilateral action taken to try to shut down Tor browser (or any of the other services used to access the dark web) in an attempt to stem terrorist financing and reduce the drug trade will most likely result in pushback from groups like Human Rights Watch and Reporters without Borders, as well as from individuals who rely on Tor to access the internet without threat of government censorship. Additionally, shutting down the dark web would have immediate negative consequences for those relying on it for safety and security. There is more to the dark web than meets the eye, and this is worthy of extensive, all-encompassing consideration on the global stage.

Five Examples to Illustrate the Benefits of the Dark Web

Daniel Wendorf and Benedikt Plass-Fleßenkämper

Daniel Wendorf is a technology writer and a PhD candidate at Technische Universität Dresden in Germany. Benedikt Plass-Fleßenkämper is a founder of the Plassma Media Agency and a freelance journalist for Spiegel Online, Zeit Online, *and* WIRED Germany.

The term "darknet" is commonly associated with evil machinations, especially because illegal darknet platforms like Silk Road and AlphaBay have attracted lots of media attention for pedalling drugs, weapons and human organs. This hidden part of the net was quickly condemned as a wicked place, with one German politician even calling it an "island of lawlessness." All of which very effectively demonstrated how many people truly do not understand what it is all about.

Is the Darknet the Internet's Dark Side?

The term darknet refers to online communication and activity that is anonymous and only accessible via Tor another special browser. Darknets use encryption technologies to establish connections between two users manually and purposefully, rather than arbitrarily. Using a computer or mobile device, one person can contact another by directly linking their two IP addresses, which allows users to communicate or exchange data without anyone looking over their shoulders. Additional contacts can be added to any private network, though each network remains cut-off from the conventional internet. Users only interact with other like-minded users in the secure space created on one of the many large and small darknets on the internet.

Generally speaking, there are many good reasons people have to have access to secure online exchange in these times of increasing surveillance. Here are a few examples of how closed networks and Tor technology can be used for good:

Whistleblowing

Edward Snowden and Chelsea Manning probably top the list of well-known whistleblowers who have disclosed questionable government machinations. Former CIA employee Snowden unveiled the US National Security Agency's (NSA) escalating global surveillance activities. Former US soldier Bradley Manning, now known as Chelsea Manning following sex-reassignment surgery, turned over half a million US war documents from Iraq and Afghanistan to the Wikileaks platform for publication. While neither Snowden nor Manning used the darknet to keep their identities a secret, they inspired other people around the globe to follow their lead and expose all kinds of wrongdoing. This is easier and safer to do if you can cover your own tracks. A program like the Tor browser can help and is used by whistleblowers worldwide.

Secure Drops for Newsrooms

Television news and newspapers depend on informants for certain types of information, informants who often prefer to remain anonymous for their own safety. Journalists are committed to protecting their sources, so every major newsroom has established a secure way people can send materials or contact staff confidentially. Dailies like Britain's the Guardian, the New York Times, and Germany's tageszeitung (taz) have created secure drops using the Tor .onion extension so users can upload documents without disclosing their IP addresses. Large NGOs such as Greenpeace also use the technology.

Systemli.org/Riseup.net

Globally many activist groups depend on secure communication channels to coordinate their activities. Regional chapters of the Chaos Computer Club hacker collective, for example, use .onion pages for all internal communication. Systemli.org touts itself as a "non-commercial provider for data-protection-friendly communication." The German initiative included protecting political activists in its mission statement, and offers e-mail, cloud and hosting services for individuals and organizations in part through .onion addresses. US counterpart Riseup.net offers similar services.

FireChat

Launched by Open Garden in 2014, the FireChat messenger service was an immediate darling of the "anonymous scene" the very same year. During the "Umbrella Revolution" in Hong Kong, the Chinese government shut down the mobile phone network in large parts of the city to block communication between activists. FireChat proved to be a good alternative communication option, as it turns any smartphone it is installed on into a communication node in a decentralized network. The app enabled thousands of demonstrators in Hong Kong to stay connected and coordinate activities despite mobile phone network shutdowns.

Facebookcorewwwi.onion

While many assume Facebook is available anywhere in the world, that is not entirely true. In some countries the site is either not accessible at all or subject to strict government controls. Facebook set up a special Tor page in 2014 to bypass censorship and blocked access.

The Deep Web

Deep web is term often associated with and misused as a synonym for the darknet. It refers to the part of the internet not discoverable by standard search engines, which do not have the technical capacities to index the websites hosted there. And while it may sound like just a marginal fraction of the world wide web, a 2001 study showed that the data volume of the deep web is anywhere from 400 to 500 times larger than that of the surface web, the publically accessible internet most users are familiar with. A large part of the net remains hidden from the general surfing public, and even government agencies find it difficult to map the activities there. Interestingly, most people are entirely unaware that they regularly use the deep web in their everyday lives. Anyone who has accessed a library catalogue online, for example, has accessed the deep web. Media holdings are not available to search engine crawlers; only registered library patrons can sign in to the catalogue, taking them into the deep web.

How to Access the Darknet: Tor Software

Originally an acronym for "the onion router," Tor is the best-known software for anonymizing data on the internet. The network that protects journalists today was originally designed to safeguard the identities of US agents and armed forces online. Cambridge University launched the project in 2000 with financial backing from the US military, and a non-profit organization took over the still quite cutting-edge technology in 2006. Today activists all over the world use Tor and other similar software to coordinate members and expose illegal or immoral activities. But in countries like China, where internet access is closely regulate and controlled, government agencies have already developed methods for shutting down Tor.

Cryptocurrency Instruments Make for Viable Investment Vehicles

United Traders

United Traders (UT) is an investment and financial services company that specializes in the development of modern, tech-driven trading solutions.

Traditional markets—equity, bonds, futures, options, Forex, etc.—provide traders with a vast selection of instruments to trade and invest in. There are seemingly no problems in switching from one market to another, if the current environment offers no trading opportunities. However, the traditional financial system is interconnected too deeply: volatility and volume are gone from virtually every marketplace. The flourishing crypto market that is still enjoying its independent nature has come to the rescue for traders. Why crypto trading is attractive and what newbies may face in this market—we are answering these questions in what follows.

2008 Crisis Aftermath

The policy pursued by central banks around the world to save the economy during the 2008 crisis aimed at pumping in liquidity has brought the financial system to a reality distortion: money has become virtually free, and rates are even negative in some countries. And these measures have had a material effect on traders active in any segment of the traditional financial system.

The US stock market is the most striking example. The bull market has been shamelessly long: if the S&P Index returns positive results by the end of the year, 2018 will be the tenth consecutive year of growth breaking the record of 1991–1999. 2017 has become the pinnacle of low volatility amid Trump's tax reform expectations: the "fear index," VIX, has been continuously breaking its record lows.

"Transitioning from Traditional Markets to Cryptocurrencies," United Traders, September 27, 2018. Reprinted by permission.

All of the above has resulted in a dry season spanning multiple years for active traders: surely, the longer the markets stay calm, the lower the volatility and trade volume. This is why, all asset classes move less aggressively, volatility declines, and it's becoming ever harder to trade big size orders. Conventional correlations disappear, past news drivers stop working, and many trading strategies die. Mistakes become more costly in this environment, making it harder to stay profitable. A calm market is not particularly bad for long-term investors (who employ the buy&hold strategy), which is why passive investing like ETFs (of which, there is a vast quantity) has become so popular in recent years. The absolute majority of actively-managed funds, however, underperform vs indexes.

In contrast to traditional markets, the crypto market has seen an explosion of interest in 2017 driving volatility to incredible highs and bringing along returns of hundreds of per cent. Therefore, no trader could have missed it as volatility is like a prey that all active traders are after. But the rise was so rapid that not everyone had a chance to participate. The continuing correction in the crypto market is an opportunity for everyone to get prepared and not miss new chances that this market will offer in the future.

Although different markets share many similarities, a trader should consider certain specifics that he will face when switching to crypto trading. Below we discuss these specifics.

Similarities Between Stocks and Cryptocurrencies

Market Psychology

Any market is driven by the balance of buyers and sellers, by their expectations and emotions. Human psychology and the accompanying behavior patterns are here to stay. You don't have to be a technology expert to start trading cryptos: price action is of the highest value and interest for traders, i.e. the chart, quotes, newsfeed, and consistent patterns; and therefore, pattern trading is applicable in this market as much as in any other market. And also you don't have to believe that cryptos and blockchain will conquer the world: the most important point is that there is a crowd whose faith may fluctuate quite wildly driving strong movements in both directions.

New Effects

When it comes to companies, traders in traditional markets closely watch quarterly reports and forecasts published by analysts and the company itself as well as M&A rumors, reshuffle of management, new contracts, drug development updates (for biotechs), etc. In case of Forex and index trading as well as government bonds traders pay attention to central bank meetings, inflation and unemployment data, economic growth indicators, etc.

Cryptocurrencies have a different specifics but they also offer a great number of newsbreaks affecting coin prices in the same fashion as news affect conventional asset classes: new project launches, new coin listings, forks, partnerships, new products, and new technology development.

Most recently, the news of SEC considering crypto ETF proposals and Goldman Sachs postponing its crypto trading desk decision (which has been eventually refuted, but after the fake news hit the feed the market fell out of bed) were of high importance for the entire market. One has to follow news like that, observe price response, and make trading decisions.

How Cryptocurrencies Are Different

Volatility and Liquidity

As mentioned, volatility is the most obvious advantage. We saw a correction in the equity market at the start of this year, which shortly boosted volatility; however, it gradually returned to a fairly low level. And no one knows how long it will stay at the current level.

It is widely accepted that 20 is the threshold for VIX, above which the market is deemed really interesting for traders; but we've been below this figure since April. For cryptocurrencies, however, a price movement of tens of per cent in a couple of days is normal even in a calm market environment. In view of insufficient mass adoption, as soon as new capital enters the market amid low liquidity prices may rise very high, which is often unjustified fundamentally.

Compared to traditional financial markets, the crypto market has relatively small number of players and less money involved, and therefore, low trading volume. Due to insufficient liquidity, buying a large quantity of coins triggers sharp and rapid price movements resulting in the average purchase price being worse than expected. This market environment basically represents an advantage for small-size traders: to a large extent, it brings higher volatility. Everything is much faster in the crypto market: the growth cycles give way to decline cycles much more frequently, and everything seems to be a fast forward play vs. conventional markets, which means money can be made (as well as lost) much faster here.

Regulations and Investor Protection

Legislators lag behind the crypto market development. Investors can feel relatively safe in the traditional markets: brokers are licensed and controlled by the regulators. Crypto exchanges, however, are unregulated, and therefore investors have no protection whatsoever. Although cryptocurrencies were initially meant to make its users independent from the government, in this particular case weak regulation is rather a drawback. No one has yet taken any responsibility for fraud, fake transactions, insider trading, and manipulations in the cryptocurrency market, which gives edge to con artists over other traders. If a company that issued tokens decides to run off with cash, investors have no legal protection.

Although fraud can also occur in traditional markets, owing to stricter controls it is rather an exception than the rule. That is to say, a regulated market is meant to provide access to assets that have been rigorously filtered. And therefore, a trader can open a chart and start trading with the understanding that what he/she sees on the chart is an actually operating company or an existing asset (we are referring to the stock market, rather than some pink sheets). In this regard the crypto market is nothing alike. That is why, traders have to be extremely careful when picking assets to trade and much more thoroughly study and research target companies as well as the management team, and background and experience of its members in order to avoid outright fraudsters.

Regulators, and first and foremost the SEC, have been closely watching and studying the crypto market recently while getting ready to establish decent supervision and control over the space. Issuers of tokens will be subject to more strict regulations as there are ever more security tokens the turnover of which is controlled by the government, which, in turn, will solve the insufficient regulation problem. In addition, more and more companies realize that issuing tokens is much cheaper and easier than issuing stock or bonds as the former eliminates middlemen, depositaries, underwriters, and other bureaucratic formalities alike.

Fundamental Valuation

In case with traditional assets, and in particular those traded in developed markets, there are public companies available in virtually every industry that one could compare valuations against in terms of various financial indicators and ratios. There are no strict and defined models available in the crypto market using which a trader could project future currency prices. In addition, new projects are hard to assess for that matter as they represent new technology that has yet to be launched or reach mass adoption.

There is also no information deficit in the traditional markets: all issuers are required to regularly file financial statements, make projections as well as update supervisory authorities on all material changes; governments publish official statistics, and an army of analysts compete in making forecasts for the majority of assets. All of the above helps investors review outlook for their investments in a particular asset.

A similar environment is just starting to form in the crypto market, which makes selecting cryptocurrencies for investing harder. One should carefully pick its information sources as there is an ever growing number of fake pundits who, while themselves having weak understanding of the technology and market, try to make money off of newbies who have no clue whom to trust. The crypto community almost exclusively uses Twitter and Telegram for communication.

Exchanges and Trading Platforms

The overall technical aspects are far from perfect too. Trading platforms are technologically deficient and inconvenient for active trading. Orders, as the platform itself, can freeze and stay inactive. Multiple open charts look awkward, and therefore one is forced to use third-party charting solutions. To some extent this flaw can be remedied by longer-term trading where seconds and fractions of a percentage point are not critical.

In case of a system failure in the traditional market, an exchange can review the incident and cancel specific trades. There is nothing like that yet in the crypto market, which increases risks for traders.

Technical support is also a problem: if a user faces troubles (incorrectly entered address or a frozen order), she is very unlikely to get a response from the support team. Another difficulty is the ever more complicated and lengthy verification procedure: sending documents in, long waits, and during periods of peak demand in the past exchanges refused to accept new clients altogether or set high minimum deposit requirements.

In addition, exchanges may be targeted by hackers. Cryptocurrency transactions are irreversible meaning that it is impossible to cancel a transfer even if it was made by a fraudster. In some cases exchanges may make up the loss, but there are no guarantees in this regard whatsoever. This is why, one should be very careful when picking a crypto exchange; we advise against depositing large amounts with a single exchange, even if that exchange is the most secure one, and recommend diversifying across multiple exchanges and transferring long-term crypto investments to cold wallets in order to reduce exchange compromise risks.

Trading Hours

Traditional exchanges are open for trading for a limited time. While you can trade futures (and Bitcoin futures too) on CME Globex and currencies on Forex virtually 24/7 but with weekends off, stock exchanges are open on weekdays only and close in the afternoon. Activity and trading volume are significantly lower during non-operating hours.

Cryptocurrency exchanges are open 24/7/365—no days off or clearing breaks, therefore a crypto trader always has access to the terminal and can make place a trade at virtually any time. On the one hand, it is a big advantage as you could choose any period for trading that suits you best, be timezone independent, and combine trading with another job, if desired.

It may also be a problem, on the other hand: the more active the trader, the more time he has to spend in front of the screen to not miss the perfect timing for entering or exiting a trade. It would be wiser to trade larger time frames to take time to rest and rejuvenate and to be less affected by smaller-scale fluctuations.

A Great Deal of New Instruments to Trade

The crypto market is very young, and therefore, new instruments are continuously born here. And as they are new, they are more likely to be less efficient vs. conventional assets that have been trading for many years by the same traders, by robots, and market makers. Meanwhile, we are witnessing the dawn of an entirely new market: new token derivatives will be created and all this taken together will provide additional volume for trading, investing, and hedging operations.

Infancy of the market also means the many coins were listed just recently and traders have insufficient historic data for analyzing and testing their strategies.

Risk Management

Risk assessment is always the most important part of the business, and it is particularly true for cryptocurrencies in view of all the above challenges. Risk management in cryptocurrency trading ought to be more strict than in traditional markets for both individual trades and total capital used in crypto trading. Stocks and currencies also exhibit sharp and unexpected price moves, of course, but more often than not, such moves are exceptions. A 5% to 10% daily change in the top coins is a non-event. It is also important to always add a significant margin when assessing risks as it may be much harder to exit at the planned price due to insufficient liquidity.

In addition, while the only risk a stock trader takes is his trading losses, a crypto trader also bears infrastructure risks, and therefore, the crypto trading capital should be much smaller than the capital used for stock market trading. The principle stays the same: do not trade with money you can't afford to lose, and this rule becomes really crucial in the crypto market.

Conclusion

In view of the above, crypto trading is not hard or complicated for traders, and for experienced traders in particular: take crypto specifics into consideration and control your risks. The infrastructure will inevitably improve over time.

As for us, using our experience and knowledge acquired over the years of active financial markets trading, we will do our best to make this transition as comfortable as possible since our crypto exchange was created by traders for traders. And this is exactly why, the interface of UT Exchange will look familiar to you, and you'll be able to trade safely and comfortably just as you would in a traditional financial market.

The Dark Web Is an Attractive Environment for Criminals

Michael Chertoff and Tobby Simon

Michael Chertoff is a former US circuit judge and served as US secretary of Homeland Security from 2005 to 2009. Tobby Simon is a founder and president of Synergia, a strategic think tank that advises private and public entities on a range of issues, from cybersecurity to supply chain risk management.

[…]

The dark Web is the portion of the deep Web that has been intentionally hidden and is inaccessible through standard Web browsers. Dark Web sites serve as a platform for Internet users for whom anonymity is essential, since they not only provide protection from unauthorized users, but also usually include encryption to prevent monitoring.

A relatively known source for content that resides on the dark Web is found in the Tor network. The Tor network is an anonymous network that can only be accessed with a special Web browser, called the Tor browser (Tor 2014a). First debuted as The Onion Routing (Tor) project in 2002 by the US Naval Research Laboratory, it was a method for communicating online anonymously. Another network, I2P, provides many of the same features that Tor does. However, I2P was designed to be a network within the Internet, with traffic staying contained in its borders. Tor provides better anonymous access to the open Internet and I2P provides a more robust and reliable "network within the network."

Usage

The ability to traverse the Internet with complete anonymity nurtures a platform ripe for what are considered illegal activities in some countries, including:

- controlled substance marketplaces;
- credit card fraud and identity theft; and
- leaks of sensitive information.

Silk Road was an online marketplace that dealt with contraband drugs, narcotics and weapons. In 2013, the US Federal Bureau of Investigation (FBI) shut down the website. But like the mythical Hydra, the website resurrected as Silk Road 2.0 within a month. It took the FBI another year to track down its administrator and servers.

It should also be noted that Tor empowers anyone who wants control over his or her online footprint. The positive value of such a tool is huge for some groups, such as whistle-blowers who report news that companies would prefer to suppress, human rights workers struggling against repressive governments and parents trying to create a safe way for their children to explore the Web.

Defining Attributes

Anonymity, from the Greek word *anonymia*, refers to the state where one's personal identity is not publicly known. Each day, our Web actions leave footprints by depositing personal data on the Internet. This information composes our digital identity—our representation in cyberspace.

Internet anonymity is guaranteed when Internet Protocol (IP) addresses cannot be tracked. Tor client software routes Internet traffic through a worldwide volunteer network of servers, hiding user's information and eluding any activities of monitoring. This makes the dark Web very appropriate for cybercriminals, who are constantly trying to hide their tracks.

The dark Web is also the preferred channel for governments to exchange documents secretly, for journalists to bypass censorship of several states and for dissidents to avoid the control of authoritarian regimes. Anonymous communications have an important place in our political and social discourse. Many individuals wish to hide their identities due to concerns about political or economic retribution.

Onion routing is a technique for anonymous communication over a computer network. Messages are repeatedly encrypted and then sent through several network nodes, called onion routers. Like someone peeling an onion, each onion router removes a layer of encryption to uncover routing instructions, and sends the message to the next router, where the process is repeated. This technique prevents intermediary nodes from knowing the origin, destination and contents of the message.

Cybercrime in the Dark Web

Peter Grabosky (2001) notes that virtual crime is not any different than crime in the real world—it is just executed in a new medium: "'Virtual criminality' is basically the same as the terrestrial crime with which we are familiar. To be sure, some of the manifestations are new. But a great deal of crime committed with or against computers differs only in terms of the medium. While the technology of implementation, and particularly its efficiency, may be without precedent, the crime is fundamentally familiar. It is less a question of something completely different than a recognizable crime committed in a completely different way."

Drugs, Weapons and Exotic Animals

Websites such as Silk Road act as anonymous marketplaces selling everything from tame items such as books and clothes, to more illicit goods such as drugs and weapons. Aesthetically, these sites appear like any number of shopping websites, with a short description of the goods, and an accompanying photograph.

Stolen Goods and Information

It is correct to assume that dedicated sites facilitate users to trade in both physical and proprietary information, including passwords and access to passwords for surface Web paid-pornography sites and PayPal passwords. PayPal Store, Creditcards for All and (Yet) Another Porn Exchange are active websites that offer such services.

Murder

The Assassination Market website is a prediction market where a party can place a bet on the date of death of a given individual, and collect a payoff if the date is "guessed" accurately. This incentivizes the assassination of individuals because the assassin, knowing when the action will take place, could profit by making an accurate bet on the time of the subject's death. Because the payoff is for knowing the date rather than performing the action of the assassination, it is substantially more difficult to assign criminal liability for the assassination. There are also websites to hire an assassin—popular ones are White Wolves and C'thuthlu.

Terrorism

The dark Web and terrorists seem to complement each other—the latter need an anonymous network that is readily available yet generally inaccessible. It would be hard for terrorists to keep up a presence on the surface Web because of the ease with which their sites could be shut down and, more importantly, tracked back to the original poster.

While the dark Web may lack the broad appeal that is available on the surface Web, the hidden ecosystem is conducive for propaganda, recruitment, financing and planning, which relates to our original understanding of the dark Web as an unregulated space.

Hacktivism

More radical critics and hacktivists occupy part of the political dissidence space. The group Anonymous, commonly associated with Occupy Wall Street and other cyber activism, is one prominent hacktivist group.

Exploit Markets

Exploits are malware based on software's vulnerabilities—before they are patched. Zero-day exploits target zero-day vulnerabilities—those for which no official patch has been released by the vendor. "Zero-day" refers to the fact that the programmer has had zero days to fix the flaw. Exploit markets serve as platforms for buying and selling zero-day exploits, and an exploit's price factors in how widely the target software is used as well as the difficulty of cracking it.

Illegal Financing Transactions

Websites such as Banker & Co. and InstaCard facilitate untraceable financial transactions through various methods. They either launder bitcoins by disguising the true origin of the transactions or give users an anonymous debit card issued by a bank. Users are also given virtual credit cards issued by trusted operators in the dark Web.

Buying stolen credit card information has never been easier. A website called Atlantic Carding offers this service, and the more you pay, the more you get. Up for grabs are business credit card accounts and even infinite credit card accounts associated with ultra-high-net-worth individuals. The user's details—name, address and so on—are available at an additional cost.

The Hidden Wiki

The main directory on the dark Web is the Hidden Wiki. It also promotes money laundering services, contract killing, cyber attacks and restricted chemicals, along with instructions to make explosives. As with other dark Web sites, the links to these sites frequently change to evade detection.

Human Experimentation

The Human Experiment was a website that detailed medical experiments claimed to have been performed on homeless people who were usually unregistered citizens. According to the website, they were picked up off the street, experimented on and then usually died. The website has been inactive since 2011.

Heist

There are many rob-to-order pages available in the dark Web, hosted by people who are good at stealing and will steal anything that you cannot afford or just do not want to pay for.

Arms Trafficking

Euroarms is a website that sells all kinds of weapons that can be delivered to your doorstep anywhere in Europe. The ammunition for these weapons is sold separately—that website has to be tracked down separately on the dark Web.

Gambling

Many popular bitcoin gambling sites block US IPs because they are afraid of prosecution from the United States, which has a tight hand on gambling in the United States. With the help of the dark Web, users of these sites can continue gambling by disguising their US IP.

Pedophilia

Pedophilia, or CP (for child pornography) as it is commonly referred to on the dark Web, is extremely accessible. Pornography is accepted on the surface Web with some regulation. The dark Web offers various types of sites and forums for those wishing to engage in pedophilia.

[…]

Monitoring the Dark Web

The dark Web, in general, and the Tor network, in particular, offer a secure platform for cybercriminals to support a vast amount of illegal activities—from anonymous marketplaces to secure means of communication, to an untraceable and difficult to shut down infrastructure for deploying malware and botnets.

As such, it has become increasingly important for security agencies to track and monitor the activities in the dark Web, focusing today on Tor networks, but possibly extending to other technologies in the near future.

Due to its intricate webbing and design, monitoring the dark Web will continue to pose significant challenges. Efforts to address it should be focused on the areas discussed below

Mapping the Hidden Services Directory

Both Tor and I2P use a domain database built on a distributed system known as a "distributed hash table," or DHT. A DHT works by having nodes in the system collaboratively take responsibility for storing and maintaining a subset of the database, which is in the form of a key-value store. Due to the distributed nature of the hidden services domain resolution, it is possible to deploy nodes in the DHT to monitor requests coming from a given domain.

Customer Data Monitoring

Security agencies could benefit from analyzing customer Web data to look for connections to non-standard domains. Depending on the level of Web usage at the customer side, this may not help in tracking down links to the dark Web, but it may still provide insights on activities hosted with rogue top-level domains. This can be done without intruding on the user's privacy as only the destinations of the Web requests need to be monitored and not who is connecting to them.

Social Site Monitoring

Sites such as Pastebin are often used to exchange contact information and addresses for new hidden services. These sites would need to be kept under constant observation to spot message exchanges containing new dark Web domains.

Hidden Service Monitoring

Most hidden services to date tend to be highly volatile and go offline very often, coming back online later under a new domain name. It is essential to get a snapshot of every new site as soon as it is spotted, for later analysis or to monitor its online activity. While crawling the clear Internet is usually an operation involving the retrieval of resources related to a site, this is not recommended in the dark Web. There is the possibility of automatically downloading content such as child pornography, the simple possession of which is considered illegal in most countries.

[...]

Conclusion

The deep Web—in particular, networks on the dark Web such as Tor—represents a viable way for malicious actors to exchange goods, legally or illegally, in an anonymous fashion.

The lack of observable activities in unconventional dark Web networks does not necessarily mean they do not exist. In fact, in agreement with the principle that inspires the dark Web, the activities are simply more difficult to spot and observe. A driving factor for the marketplace is critical mass. Operators in the dark Web are unlikely to need a high level of stealth unless the consequences, if they are discovered, are sufficiently severe. It is conceivable that sites may come online at specific times, have a brief window of trading, then disappear, making them more difficult to investigate.

Recent revelations about wide-scale nation-state monitoring of the Internet and recent arrests of cybercriminals behind sites hosted in the dark Web are starting to lead to other changes. It would not be surprising to see the criminal underbelly becoming more fragmented into alternative dark nets or private networks, further complicating the job of investigators.

The dark Web has the potential to host an increasingly large number of malicious services and activities and, unfortunately, it will not be long before new large marketplaces emerge. Security researchers have to remain vigilant and find new ways to spot upcoming malicious services to deal with new phenomena as quickly as possible.

Cryptocurrency Valuation Is Less Than Reliable

David Veksler

David Veksler is a writer and director of technology at the Foundation for Economic Education. He worked as an information systems architect at Match.com, Education First, and Liberty.me.

What is the real market value of cryptocurrencies like Bitcoin? The numbers used to explain the performance of Bitcoin and other cryptocurrencies are less meaningful than most assume.

Cryptocurrencies are not exactly like stocks, and cryptocurrency exchanges do not work like traditional securities markets. As a result, many crypto-asset investment strategies based on conventional definitions of market share, capitalization, volatility, and trading volume are deeply flawed. Misleading numbers mean that cryptocurrency valuation and adoption is poorly understood, which creates a false perception by the media and investors about cryptocurrencies such as Bitcoin. One implication of this analysis is that Bitcoin has captured the vast majority of the long-term upside in the cryptocurrency market despite having about half the nominal market share.

Most cryptocurrencies and crypto exchanges manipulate numbers in ways that publicly traded companies and traditional exchanges like NASDAQ and NYSE wouldn't dream of. As a result, "market capitalization" and "trading volume" are at best rough and relative measures of cryptocurrency adoption. Even when intentional manipulation is not involved, crypto-asset markets fundamentally just do not function like securities markets. It's important to understand these differences to asses the state of cryptocurrency and crypto asset adoption.

"Three Key Differences Between Traditional and Crypto Markets," by David Veksler, December 2, 2018. Reprinted by permission.

Let's look at three important differences between how cryptocurrencies and traditional securities markets work:

Cryptocurrency Valuation Comes Almost Entirely from Speculation on Future Adoption

The first major difference between Bitcoin and securities is that the vast majority of the market value of Bitcoin comes from the speculation on future adoption. Today, Bitcoin is being used as practical money and a store of value in countries by a few million users. Bitcoin is already useful and superior to government-issued money in countries suffering from hyperinflation such as Venezuela and Zimbabwe. Bitcoin is also used to bypass currency controls in China and India. Even in these cases, Bitcoin competes with other less-than-legal alternatives, due to the lack of ecosystem adoption and government prohibitions. In developed countries, Bitcoin is only used by its most devoted followers, as the traditional financial system is still far easier to use.

However, the number of current Bitcoin use cases is vastly overshadowed by expectations that it will supplement assets such as precious metals and fiat currencies such as the dollar in the future. In short, the majority of Bitcoin's value derives from speculation on the future adoption of Bitcoin as a practical payment network. The problem is that investors have very little evidence to predict the future value of Bitcoin. The scope of possibilities includes Bitcoin failing entirely, becoming a small but viable alternative in specific use cases, supplementing gold and dollars as a viable substitute, or becoming the world's new reserve currency.

One of the signs of this lack of certainty is the percentage of Bitcoin traded daily. Bitcoin's daily volume—as of November 2018—is worth $7.3 billion out of a $75 billion valuation, or about 10%. Apple's volume is $6.2 billion out of an $850 billion valuation—or about .7%. Bitcoin is much more volatile than stocks—it has more than ten times the volatility of a typical security, and virtually all other non-pegged cryptocurrencies are far more volatile than Bitcoin. People hold Apple stock because it has a track record of successful products and loyal customers whereas most Bitcoin holders own to speculate on future adoption and price growth.

Cryptocurrency Markets Have Thin Order Books Compared to Traditional Securities Exchanges

Another important difference between crypto and traditional markets is the size of their order books. A traditional stock like Apple is transacted on a single exchange, with tens of millions of stocks available to trade daily from many thousands of buyers and seller. As a result, securities markets like NYSE and NASDAQ have minimal slippage—they can efficiently process large orders and the current market price.

Bitcoin owners, on the other hand, keep most of their assets in offline wallets, with only a small percentage on vulnerable markets (which are often hacked, defrauded, etc). As a result, a million-dollar Bitcoin order might have a major effect on a given exchange, with a ripple effect on other exchanges. For example, the sale of Bitcoins formerly held by Mt Gox caused dramatic price drops, even though only 1% of the outstanding Bitcoin were up for sale. This effect is far more pronounced with other cryptocurrencies, which explains why $500 billion was wiped out during 2018.

Here is a hypothetical example:

Suppose that I create a new "Vex Coin" with an initial quantity of 1 million coins. I pay "ABC Exchange" 10 Bitcoin to list my count and get my friend Joe to buy 1 "Vex Coin" for $100 dollars worth of Bitcoin. My brand-new coin is now worth $100 million dollars, which at time of writing would put it at #50 in the CoinMarketCap list of all cryptocurrencies. I just created a $100 million market cap with a $100 investment! Now, suppose I issue 9 million additional coins. Vex Coin now has a $1 billion valuation!

A report by the Blockchain Transparency Institute claims that 70 of the top 100% exchanges are faking volume numbers, either by lying outright or wash trading. Wash trading strategies include free trades, paying customers a small percentage to place trades, or secretly running bots on their own exchange masquerading as real customers. These "market maker bots" are a very common way to launch a new exchange and create fake volume in order to drive up rankings of both exchanges and coins.

The relatively greater difficulty in faking Bitcoin prices and volume is why I believe that Bitcoin has captured nearly all the value in the cryptocurrency space, despite the fact that its nominal share of crypto-asset market capital has been as low as 30% in 2018. In fact, I believe that the alignment of Bitcoin's (or whatever coin emerges as the leader) nominal market share to its true market value will be one of the key sign of maturation in the crypto-asset space.

The Valuation of Crypto Assets Is Backed by Relatively Little Real-World Investment

The third important difference between crypto and traditional securities is the ratio of investment cost to market cap. The total value of a corporation's stock is based on investors belief in its profit-making potential in the future. This profit-making ability is enabled by the money invested to buy its stock. Take a company like Apple, with a market cap of $850 billion. The majority of that valuation represents created wealth—that is, Apple's stock offering was for a far smaller amount than its current valuation. Nevertheless, investors have given Apple hundreds of billions to fund its growth over the last several decades by buying its stock. In recent years, IPOs have averaged a 21% return over the last few years, which is a healthy but modest return on investment. Compare this to Bitcoin:

Bitcoin is an open network, not a private entity, so its market cap is the total value of all Bitcoins at the current market price, and the investment cost is the total investment in the Bitcoin ecosystem. Currently (November 28, 2018) sites that track the "market cap" of cryptocurrencies like coinmarketcap.com report a market capitalization for Bitcoin of $73 billion. We have no way to track the total amount of fiat currency (i.e. dollars) spent to buy that Bitcoin, but we know exactly how much profit (in Bitcoin) miners have made from mining Bitcoin. Bitcoin mining is a competitive market process, and profit margins are thin or non-existent, so we can assume that most minted Bitcoins were traded for fiat (dollars) to pay for expenses, such as buying mining hardware, and electricity. If Bitcoin miners sold Bitcoin on the same day they mined it to pay for operating expenses, they would have earned $5.3 billion. This is 7% of Bitcoin's market cap.

Mining is only a part of the Bitcoin ecosystem—exchanges like Kraken and Coinbase, and Gemini and merchant services such as Bitpay have invested in the Bitcoin ecosystem, but these are not large companies. In short, Bitcoin's value on paper is backed by relatively little investment in its ecosystem.

This is not a bad thing if you believe in the world-changing potential of cryptocurrencies. However, it is important to understand the relationship of a cryptocurrency to the resources it has at its disposal. For example, Litecoin, with a valuation of nearly $2 billion dollars has two full-time developers.

Bitcoin Is Not Vaporware, But Most Other Cryptocurrencies Are

There are hundreds of developers working on blockchain ecosystem development at companies such as Blockstream, Bitpay, Coinbase, Gemini, Satoshi Labs, and others. However, Apple has 132,000 employees, and revenue of $266 billion to back up its $850 billion market cap. When cryptocurrencies were worth $800+ billion this January, I would guess that there were about 100 mostly volunteer Bitcoin Core contributors and a few thousand people employed in Bitcoin ecosystem startups.

Bitcoin is the best-case scenario. The majority of cryptocurrencies are vaporware, with virtually no technical teams. Bitcoin uses a proof-of-work coin-creation model, whereas the majority of coins (such as ERC20 coins) use a proof-of-stake model, which does not use mining, or involves minimal mining. Their mining costs are zero, though they might still have R&D, personnel, marketing costs, etc. Most cryptocurrencies are get-rich-quick schemes, with little vision, technical innovation, or market adoption.

A typical coin founder team contracts out the technical work of creating a new coin and has no technical staff or ongoing development ecosystem. Their market cap is based on inflated trade volumes and their coin minting strategy is designed solely to prop up the price long enough for all the founders to realize their profits before the price collapses.

To take a typical example, look up a cryptocurrencies' GitHub account, which records the contributions that developers are making to it. Here is Bitcoin Gold. There is typically a burst of activity around the launch date, followed by a lot of marketing hype and little or no technical work. Most cryptocurrencies have no paid developers or open-source developer community.

Corporations can spend money on technical innovation, and I suspect that many cryptocurrency investors assume that the cryptocurrency valuations reflect an ability to deliver on their promise. The reality is that exchange manipulation and inflated volume numbers mean that real demand for most cryptocurrencies is very low. The founding teams cannot fund development by selling their closely-held stash because the coins price would collapse before more than a tiny fraction was sold.

As a result, most projects have only a few people, and no ongoing technical development. Based on my review of GitHub open source code contributions to top cryptocurrencies, the majority of projects have zero dedicated blockchain architects, and in fact zero full-time contributors of any kind. Once you get past the top currencies such as Bitcoin, Ethereum, Stellar, etc, most coins have few developers and little activity.

Solutions

The above criticism may seem like I'm bearish on cryptocurrencies, but that's not at all my intention. I want to help you separate the hype and speculation around cryptocurrencies from the underlying fundamentals. The primary drivers of cryptocurrency price stability will be adoption for non-speculative purposes and an understanding of the fundamentals driving Bitcoin adoption. We need to understand the matured of the blockchain ecosystem in order to have a measured and calm response to currency volatility and retain a positive outlook on the future.

The Three Stages of Crypto Ecosystem Maturation

Cryptocurrency development will likely proceed in three stages: discovery, infrastructure, and adoption. The discovery stage was from 2008-2013 when the community identified the basic concepts and tools of cryptocurrencies. The infrastructure stage started around the time that people realized the need to build alternatives to the failed Mt Gox exchange in 2013. The current infrastructure phase involves the creation of an ecosystem which provides foolproof custody solutions for consumers, trusted intermediaries, and a diverse network of vendors who accept Bitcoin. Once a mature infrastructure is in place for cryptocurrencies, the stage will be set for adoption.

Unfortunately, real innovations in cryptocurrency space are being hidden behind the veil of speculative hype. For example, over the last year, over half of Bitcoin users adopted a new Segwit address format that increases security and transaction capacity. Lightning Network just reached $1M BTC capacity and 4,000 Nodes. This is a second-layer Bitcoin network that has enough capacity for every single human being to use his own Bitcoin wallet—something that no other cryptocurrency can credibly claim.

A meaningful assessment of Bitcoin's value lies in understanding the ecosystem's readiness for institutional and consumer adoption. The ecosystem is still extremely immature, and the tools are nowhere near ready for a typical consumer, but that landscape is rapidly changing and setting the stage for mass consumer adoption.

The Dark Web Provides Unique Advantages for Criminals

Pierluigi Paganini

Pierluigi Paganini is a writer and cyber security analyst. He is CTO at Cybaze Enterprise, editor in chief at Cyber Defense Magazine, *and a member of the European Union Agency for Network and Information Security.*

The Dark web is a privileged place for cyber criminals that, under specific conditions, could operate in anonymity.

The United Nation's Office on Drugs and Crime (UNODC) has published its annual report that contains a specific mention to the illicit trade of goods and drugs in this hidden part of the web.

The crooks seem to be one step ahead of many countries' law enforcement agencies that in many cases are not able to target black markets in the dark web.

Illegal activities in the Dark Web are growing, an increasing number of criminals is abusing anonymizing networks such as the Tor Network and I2P.

"Drug supply via the Internet, including via the anonymous online marketplace, the 'dark net,' may have increased in recent years. This raises concerns in terms of the potential of the 'dark net' to attract new populations of users by facilitating access to drugs in both developed and developing countries," states the report.

The Europol made a similar call in a 2014 report when addressing the shortcoming in its capabilities of dealing with online drug dealing.

"Law enforcement should build technical capabilities in order to support technical investigations into subjects using Darknets, in accordance with relevant legislation," states the law enforcement agency.

"Law Enforcement and the Dark Web: A Never-Ending Battle," by Pierluigi Paganini, INFOSEC Resources, July 19, 2016. Reprinted by permission.

When dealing with the growth of illegal activities in the Dark Web, legislation, technical abilities and capacity building are essential components of a strategy that must be shared by law enforcement agencies worldwide.

Law enforcement bodies in many countries are still not in a position to deal effectively with the illegal activities that leverage infrastructures in the Dark Web. The anonymity of the actors and jurisdictional issues are the most common issues that obstacle their activity.

In many cases, technical difficulties requested the involvement of undercover agents to infiltrate black marketplaces to identify its operators.

The purchasing of drugs via the "dark net" raises concerns regarding the potential of the "dark net" to attract the ordinary crime; black markets are crucial facilitators for multiple illegal activities. At the same time, we are assisting to a significant increment in the number of transactions related the payment of illegal goods, bitcoins and other crypto-currencies are becoming the norm in many black markets.

The United Nation's Office on Drugs and Crime (UNODC) report also cites a global survey of more than 100,000 Internet users (75 percent of whom had purchased illegal drugs) in 50 countries in late 2014.

The survey confirms an increase in the number of users purchasing drugs via the Internet; the percentage had increased from 1.2 percent in 2000 to 4.9 percent in 2009, 16.4 percent in 2013 and 25.3 per cent in 2014. It is interesting to note that the number of Internet users that purchased drugs via the "dark net" is also increased.

Below are reported the key findings of The Global Drug Survey 2016 report published this year.

- "More people shopping on the dark net, more people using MDMA & experiencing harm, synthetic cannabinoids the most dangerous drugs in the world. "

- Globally almost in 1 in 10 participants (9.3%) reported ever buying drugs off the darknet with those reporting last year dark-net purchase rising from 4.5% to 6.7%.
- MDMA, cannabis, new or novel substances (including 2C-B and DMT) and LSD are the drugs most commonly bought
- 5% of respondents stated that they did not consume drugs before accessing them through darknet markets

Analyzing data related to English-speaking countries, it is possible to observe an increase between 2015 and 2016 in UK, Ireland, US, Canada. The situation is quite stable in Australia and New Zealand.

The intelligence agencies that appear to be the most aggressive when dealing drugs and other illegal activities on the Dark Web are the FBI and the NCA, let's see their activity in detail.

The National Crime Agency in the Dark Web

The dark web is a dark zone for law enforcement agencies worldwide, in this hidden portion of the web crooks can buy and sell drugs, weapons, stolen data, it is also considered a facilitator for the child pornography. At the end of 2015, the British law enforcement and intelligence agencies, including the GCHQ and the National Crime Agency (NCA), have created a new unit, the *Joint Operations Cell* (JOC), that will specifically address the cybercrime.

The mission of the new unit will be initially focused on tackling online child sexual exploitation as explained in the official statement issued by the NSA.

"An NCA and GCHQ co-located Joint Operations Cell (JOC) opens officially today. The unit brings together officers from the two agencies to focus initially on tackling online child sexual exploitation," states the press release published by the NSA.

The British Government is always at the forefront in the fight against online child sexual exploitation, in December 2014 the UK Prime Minister David Cameron announced the plan for the creation of a unit of cyber experts that will be involved in the investigation of crimes exploiting the dark web.

Cameron revealed that national intelligence agencies would join the efforts to track and arrest online abusers and pedophiles, he also added that the UK Government would have greater powers for online monitoring of suspects. According to UK authorities, up to 1,300 children are exposed to online abuse from pedophiles, and it is the tip of the iceberg, for this reason, it is a moral and social obligation to fight this illegal practice.

Cameron explained the strategy of the British Government at the #WeProtectChildren online global summit in London, announcing the creation of a new unit composed of members from the GCHQ and the National Crime Agency (NCA).

One of the greatest challenges of law enforcement that operates against online pedophiles is to track them even online even if they make large use of anonymizing networks like Tor.

"The so-called 'dark-net' is increasingly used by pedophiles to view sickening images. I want them to hear loud and clear: we are shining a light on the web's darkest corners; if you are thinking of offending, there will be nowhere for you to hide," Cameron said.

The JOC will have the ambitious plan to fight any kind of online criminal activity.

"The Joint Operations Cell will increase our ability to identify and stop serious criminals, as well as those involved in child sexual exploitation and abuse online. This is a challenging task as we must detect them while they attempt to hide in the mass of data. We are committed to ensuring no part of the internet, including the dark web, can be used with impunity by criminals to conduct their illegal acts," explained the GCHQ Director Robert Hannigan.

The FBI and the Dark Web ...
the Never-Ending Story

In July 2015, two individuals from New York had been charged with online child pornography crimes after visiting a hidden service on the Tor network.

The Federal Bureau of Investigation (FBI) identified them by using a hacking tool that allowed law enforcement to de-anonymize the suspects while surfing on the Tor network.

After months of speculations and hypotheses on the mysterious tool, court documents reviewed by Motherboard provided more information on the hacking technique exploited by the FBI to identify the suspects.

The document confirmed that it was the first time that the FBI conducted such an extended operation against Tor users, according to the court documents, the FBI agents monitored a bulletin board hidden service launched in August 2014, named Playpen. Playpen was a hidden service used for in the dark web for "the advertisement and distribution of child pornography," it reached in just one year over 200,000 users, with over 117,000 total posts mainly containing child pornography content. The FBI agents were able to discover nearly 1300 IP addresses belonging to the visitors.

The FBI seized the server where the Playpen service was hosted belonging to a web host located in North Carolina and used it is a sort of watering hole attack to track its visitors. The FBI operation leveraged on the network investigative technique (NIT) to obtain the IP addresses of the Playpen users.

The technique was not new; the FBI used the NIT to de-anonymize Tor users also in previous operations. On December 22th, 2014 Mr. Joseph Gross retained the assistance of Dr. Ashley Podhradsky, Dr. Matt Miller, and Mr. Josh Stroschein to provide the testimony as the expert in the process against pedos on Tor.

The suspects were accused in federal court in Omaha of viewing and possessing child pornography.

To better understand what the NIT is, let me share the explanation provided by the cyber security expert H.D. Moore, who developed it.

"The NIT was a Flash-based application that was developed by H.D. Moore and was released as part of Metasploit. The NIT, or more formally, Metasploit Decloaking Engine was designed to provide the real IP address of web users, regardless of proxy settings," stated the forensic report.

According to the court documents, the investigators were informed that there were three servers containing contraband images that the FBI found and took offline in November of 2012.

Authorities used the server as bait for online pedos, the FBI placed the NIT on the servers and used them to de-anonymize TOR users accessing the illegal content. With this technique, the FBI identified the IP addresses of visitors.

The NIT technique was also used in 2011 by agents running the "Operation Torpedo," when agents deployed the script on seized servers to track visitors.

According to court documents related to the Playpen, the version of NIT currently used by the FBI is different from the one used in the past during the Operation Torpedo.

Colin Fieman that is defending Jay Michaud, a Vancouver public schools administration worker arrested by the FBI right after the FBI closed "Playpen," believe that many other users of the illegal service will be arrested due to the use of the network investigative technique (NIT).

"Fifteen-hundred or so of these cases are going to end up getting filed out of the same, underlying investigation," Colin Fieman, told Motherboard in a phone interview. Fieman, who is representing Jay Michaud, a Vancouver teacher arrested in July 2015, said his estimate comes from what "we've seen in terms of the discovery. There will probably be an escalating stream of these [cases] in the next six months or so."

When dealing with hacking tools like the NIT to de-anonymize Tor users, it is important to consider that law enforcement agencies like the FBI used only one warrant to hack computers of unknown suspects all over the world.

This is considered not legal by privacy advocates, including the defense of the suspects in the Playpen case that speculates the

US government was running a dragnet surveillance not allowed by national law.

Earlier 2016, a judge ruled that the FBI's actions did not constitute "outrageous conduct," but now a new order got out and obligated the FBI to disclose all the entire source code of the NIT investigative component.

Michaud's lawyers requested to get access to the NIT code used by the FBI since September, but they hadn't obtained it until January when the expert defense Tsyrklevitch received the code.

Tsyrklevitch argues that the provided code was incomplete, the parts related to the exploited were not included in the NIT component he analyzed.

"This component is essential to understanding whether there were other components that the Government caused to run on Mr. Michaud's computer, beyond the one payload that the Government has provided," Michaud's lawyers wrote.

Conclusion

Darknet and covert channels will continue to be abused by crooks making hard law enforcement investigations. Tools like the NIT could support Government activities, but represent a potential threat to users' privacy.

Although the FBI and other law enforcement agencies have been lauded for their efforts in the fight against the threat actors in the dark web, preventing the abuses of anonymizing networks is still a great challenge.

For this reason, governments and police bodies are training a new generation of agents that is mastering new technology, including anonymizing network.

The fight against crooks in the Dark Web needs a deep technological knowledge and the adoption of HUMINT.

The Dark Web Is a Threat That Must Be Addressed

Europol

Europol is the European Union's law enforcement agency. It is headquartered in The Hague and aims to support a safer European Union for all citizens.

Today, May 29 2018, law enforcement from 28 countries across the globe met at Europol headquarters in The Hague to share knowledge and expertise and discuss a coordinated approach to tackling crime on the dark web. Experts from Eurojust, the European Commission, the European Monitoring Centre for Drugs and Drug Addiction (EMCDDA) and INTERPOL also contributed to the event.

Europol, through the European Cybercrime Centre (EC3), has been supporting the investigation of criminal marketplaces on the dark web for some years by sharing tools, tactics, and techniques. The dark web hosts many of the more critical marketplaces for several criminal organisations and individual illegal activities in Europe and around the world. Due to its structural specificities—the possibility to buy and sell anonymously and the fact that it is a digital space that knows no national borders—it is a fertile environment for criminals.

In recent years several successful coordinated investigations were able to take down some of the largest dark web markets, undermining the assets exploited by criminals. In particular, in summer 2017 joint operations led by the US FBI and the Dutch National Police, with the support of Europol and other law enforcement partners, shut down Alphabay and Hansa, two of the largest marketplaces responsible for the trading of over 350 000 illicit goods like drugs, firearms and cybercrime tools, such

"Crime on the Dark Web: Law Enforcement Coordination Is the Only Cure," European Union Agency for Law Enforcement Cooperation, May 29, 2018. Reprinted by permission.

as malware. In these specific marketplaces, where bitcoins were the dominant payment method, different types of illegal goods and criminal services were sold, even though more than two thirds of transactions were for illicit drugs and chemical substances.

Owing to the success of these operations, the volume of transactions has decreased and some traders have left the dark web platform due to anxiety, uncertainty and the risks regarding the level of anonymity. After the takedown operations, many vendors, who had their shop closed twice in short succession, were not inclined to open them again, while the distrust between vendors and buyers has increased.

Dedicated Dark Web Team

One of Europol's initiatives is to create a coordinated law enforcement approach to tackle crime on the dark web with the participation of law enforcement agencies from across EU Member States, operational third parties as well as other relevant partners, such as Eurojust.

In order to achieve this goal, Europol has established a dedicated Dark Web Team to work together with EU partners and law enforcement globally to reduce the size of this underground illegal economy. It will deliver a complete, coordinated approach: sharing information, providing operational support and expertise in different crime areas and the development of tools, tactics, and techniques to conduct dark web investigations and identify top threats and targets. The team also aims to enhance joint technical and investigative actions, organise training and capacity-building initiatives, together with prevention and awareness-raising campaigns—a 360° strategy against criminality on the dark web.

A shared commitment across the global community and a coordinated approach by law enforcement agencies proved their effectiveness last year and are essential going forward. The scale of the assembly at Europol today demonstrated the global commitment to continued work of this nature and to jointly tackling the use of the dark web as a means to commit crime.

This is the primary reason why Europol has decided to create a new Dark Web Investigations Team embedded within its European Cybercrime Centre.

Chief Commissioner Ivaylo Spiridonov, Director of the Bulgarian General Directorate Combatting Organised Crime, delivered the opening remarks on behalf of the current Presidency of the Council of the EU and highlighted that "Today's expert assembly will further enhance the law enforcement's ability to find sustainable solutions and a common coordinated approach to respond to criminality on the dark web."

"The event also marks the official launch of the new Europol Dark Web Team which will provide operational and technical support to law enforcement in thwarting criminality on the dark web in a coordinated and multidisciplinary manner," added Catherine De Bolle, Executive Director of Europol.

In 2010 the European Union (EU) set up a four-year Policy Cycle to ensure greater continuity in the fight against serious international and organised crime. In March 2017 the Council of the EU decided to continue the EU Policy Cycle for organised and serious international crime for the 2018–2021 period. This multiannual Policy Cycle aims to tackle the most significant threats posed by organised and serious international crime to the EU in a coherent and methodological manner. This is achieved by improving and strengthening cooperation between the relevant services of EU Member States, institutions and agencies, as well as non-EU countries and organisations, including the private sector where relevant. Cybercrime is one of the priorities of the Policy Cycle.

Organizations to Contact

The editors have compiled the following list of organizations concerned with the issues debated in this book. The descriptions are derived from materials provided by the organizations. All have publications or information available for interested readers. This list was compiled on the date of publication of the present volume; the information provided here may change. Be aware that many organizations take several weeks or longer to respond to inquiries, so allow as much time as possible.

The American Civil Liberties Union (ACLU)

125 Broad Street, 18th Floor
New York, NY 10004
phone: (212) 549-2500
website: www.aclu.org

For nearly one hundred years, the ACLU has worked in courts, legislatures, and communities to defend and preserve the individual rights and liberties that the Constitution and the laws of the United States guarantee everyone.

Center for Internet Security (CIS)

31 Tech Valley Drive
East Greenbush, NY 12061
phone: (518) 266-3460
website: www.cisecurity.org

The Center for Internet Security, Inc. (CIS) is a nonprofit entity that harnesses the power of a global IT community to safeguard private and public organizations against cyber threats. The *CIS Controls* and *CIS Benchmarks* are the global standards and recognized best practices for securing IT systems and data against the most pervasive attacks. These proven guidelines are continuously refined and verified by a volunteer global community of experienced IT professionals.

Constitutional Rights Foundation (CRF)
601 S. Kingsley Drive
Los Angeles, CA 90005
phone: (213) 487-5590
website: www.crf-usa.org

CRF is a nonprofit, nonpartisan, community-based organization dedicated to educating America's young people about the importance of civic participation in a democratic society. Under the guidance of a Board of Directors chosen from the worlds of law, business, government, education, the media, and the community, CRF develops, produces, and distributes programs and materials to teachers, students, and public-minded citizens all across the nation.

Digital Media Association (DiMA)
1050 17th Street NW, Suite 520
Washington, DC 20036
phone: (202) 639-9509
email: info@dima.org
website: www.digmedia.org

DiMA is the ambassador for the digital media industry: webcasters, online media, digital services, and technology innovators. DiMA is the leading advocate for a stable legal environment in which to build ideas into industries and inventions into profits.

European Cyber Security Organization (ECSO)
10 Rue Montoyer
1000 – Brussels
Belgium
phone: +32(0)2 777 02 50
email: media@ecs-org.eu
website: www.ecs-org.eu

The European Cyber Security Organisation (ECSO) is a fully self-financed not-for-profit organization under the Belgian law, which was established in June 2016. ECSO represents the industry-led contractual counterpart to the European Commission for the implementation of the Cyber Security contractual Public-Private Partnership (cPPP).

First Amendment Center—Vanderbilt University
John Seigenthaler Center
1207 18th Avenue S.
Nashville, TN 37212
phone: (615) 727-1600
email: firstamendmentcenter@newseum.org
website: www.firstamendmentcenter.org

The First Amendment Center supports the First Amendment and builds understanding of its core freedoms through education, information, and entertainment. The center serves as a forum for the study and exploration of free-expression issues, including freedom of speech, press, and religion, and the rights to assemble and to petition the government.

Information Security Forum (ISF)
42-50 Hersham Road
Walton-on-Thames
Surrey KT12 1RZ
United Kingdom
phone: (347) 767-6772
email: steve.durbin@securityforum.org
website: www.securityforum.org

The Information Security Forum (ISF) is an independent, not-for-profit organization with a membership comprising many of the world's leading organizations featured on the Fortune 500 and Forbes 2000 lists. The ISF provides members with a trusted and confidential environment within which their in-depth knowledge and practical experience can be shared.

Information Systems Security Association (ISSA)
1964 Gallows Road, Suite 310
Vienna, VA 22182
phone: (703) 382-8205
email: memberservices@issa.org
website: www.issa.org

The Information Systems Security Association (ISSA) is a not-for-profit, international organization of information security professionals and practitioners. It provides educational forums, publications, and peer interaction opportunities that enhance the knowledge, skill, and professional growth of its members.

The SANS Institute
11200 Rockville Pike, Suite 200
North Bethesda, MD 20852
phone: (301) 654-7267
email: info@sans.org
website: www.sans.org

The SANS Institute was established in 1989 as a cooperative research and education organization. A range of individuals, from auditors and network administrators to chief information security officers, share the lessons they learn and jointly find solutions to the challenges they face. At the heart of SANS are the many security practitioners in varied global organizations from corporations to universities working together to help the entire information security community.

United States Department of Homeland Security
2707 Martin Luther King Jr. Avenue SE
Washington, DC 20528
phone: (202) 282-8000
email: mediainquiry@hq.dhs.gov
website: www.dhs.gov

The Department of Homeland Security has a vital mission: to secure the United States from the many threats it faces. This requires the dedication of more than 240,000 employees in jobs that range from aviation and border security to emergency response, from cybersecurity analyst to chemical facility inspector.

World Wide Web Consortium (W3C)

W3C/MIT
32 Vassar Street
Room 32-386
Cambridge, MA 02139
phone: (617) 253-2613
email: membership@w3.org
website: www.w3.org

The World Wide Web Consortium (W3C) is an international community where member organizations and a full-time staff work together to develop and promote a sustainable system of web standards. W3C's mission is to lead the web to its full potential.

Bibliography

Books

Jamie Bartlett, *The Dark Net: Inside the Digital Underworld.* Brooklyn, NY: Melville House Publishing, 2014.

Yochai Benkler, Robert Faris, and Hal Roberts, *Network Propaganda: Manipulation, Disinformation, and Radicalization in American Politics.* New York, NY: Oxford University Press, 2018.

Kip Boyle, *Fire Doesn't Innovate: The Executive's Practical Guide to Thriving in the Face of Evolving Cyber Risks.* Austin, TX: Lioncrest Publishing, 2019.

Marcus J. Carey and Jennifer Jin, *Tribe of Hackers: Cybersecurity Advice from the Best Hackers in the World.* Austin, TX: Threatcare Press, 2019.

John P. Carlin, *Dawn of the Code War: America's Battle Against Russia, China, and the Rising Global Cyber Threat.* New York, NY: Hachette Book Group, 2018.

Michael Chertoff, *Exploding Data: Reclaiming Our Cyber Security in the Digital Age.* New York, NY: Atlantic Monthly Press, 2018.

Richard Clarke, *Cyber War: The Next Threat to National Security and What to Do About It.* New York, NY: HarperCollins, 2010.

Marc Goodman, *Future Crimes: Inside the Digital Underground and the Battle for Our Connected World.* New York, NY: Random House, 2015.

Lance Henderson, *TOR and the Dark Art of Anonymity: How to Be Invisible from NSA Spying.* Scotts Valley, CA: CreateSpace Independent Publishing Platform, 2015.

Douglas W. Hubbard and Richard Seiersen, *How to Measure Anything in Cybersecurity Risk*. Hoboken, NJ: John Wiley & Sons, Inc., 2016.

Kathleen Hall Jamieson, *Cyberwar: How Russian Hackers and Trolls Helped Elect a President*. New York, NY: Oxford University Press, 2018.

Fred Kaplan, *Dark Territory: The Secret History of Cyber War*. New York, NY: Simon and Schuster, 2016.

Herbert Lin and Amy Zegart, eds., *Bytes, Bombs, and Spies: The Strategic Dimensions of Offensive Cyber Operations*. Washington, DC: The Brookings Institution, 2018.

Michael Melone, *Think Like a Hacker: A SysAdmin's Guide to Cybersecurity*. New York, NY: Bitlatch Books, 2017.

Evan J. Rodgers, *What Is the Dark Web?: The Truth About the Hidden Part of the Internet*. Scotts Valley, CA: CreateSpace Independent Publishing Platform, 2015.

David E. Sanger, *The Perfect Weapon: War, Sabotage, and Fear in the Cyber Age*. New York, NY: Broadway Books, 2018.

P. W. Singer and Allan Friedman, *Cybersecurity and Cyberwar: What Everyone Needs to Know*. New York, NY: Oxford University Press, 2014.

Periodicals and Internet Sources

Thomas Brewster, "This Insane Map Shows All the Beauty and Horror of the Dark Web," *Forbes*, March 13, 2018. https://www.forbes.com/sites/thomasbrewster/2018/03/13/dark-web-map-6000-webpages/#59d9b9b318e7.

Kate Conger, "WTF Is the Dark Web?" *TechCrunch*, October 30, 2016. https://techcrunch.com/2016/10/30/wtf-is-the-dark-web/.

Andy Greenberg, "Feds Dismantled the Dark Web Drug Trade—But It's Already Rebuilding," *WIRED*, May 9, 2019.

https://www.wired.com/story/dark-web-drug-takedowns-deepdotweb-rebound/.

William Langewiesche, "Welcome to the Dark Net, a Wilderness Where Invisible World Wars Are Fought and Hackers Roam Free," *Vanity Fair*, October 2016. https://www.vanityfair.com/news/2016/09/welcome-to-the-dark-net.

Nate Lord, "What Is Cyber Security? Definition, Best Practices, and More," *Digital Guardian: Data Insider*, May 15, 2019. https://digitalguardian.com/blog/what-cyber-security.

Dan Patterson, "How to Safely Access and Navigate the Dark Web," *TechRepublic*, March 11, 2019. https://www.techrepublic.com/article/how-to-safely-access-and-navigate-the-dark-web/.

Tim Scarapani, "The Dark Web Is Still a Huge, Difficult Problem," *Forbes*, June 28, 2016. https://www.forbes.com/sites/timsparapani/2016/06/28/the-dark-web-is-still-a-huge-difficult-problem/#1ccac2d065b1.

Bruce Schneier, "There's No Good Reason to Trust Blockchain Technology," *WIRED*, February 6, 2019. https://www.wired.com/story/theres-no-good-reason-to-trust-blockchain-technology/.

Justin Sherman, "How to Regulate the Internet Without Becoming a Dictator," *Foreign Policy*, February 18, 2019. https://foreignpolicy.com/2019/02/18/how-to-regulate-the-internet-without-becoming-a-dictator-uk-britain-cybersecurity-china-russia-data-content-filtering/.

Tom Simonite, "The Surprising Light Side of the Dark Web," *MIT Technology Review*, March 18, 2016. https://www.technologyreview.com/s/601073/the-surprising-light-side-of-the-dark-web/.

Derek Thompson, "Is This the Beginning of the End of the Bitcoin Bubble?" *Atlantic*, January 16, 2018. https://www.theatlantic.com/business/archive/2018/01/bitcoin-bubble-pop/550601/.

Kaveh Waddell, "How Did Cybersecurity Become So Political?" *Atlantic*, February 2, 2017. https://www.theatlantic.com/technology/archive/2017/02/how-did-cybersecurity-become-so-political/515349/.

Index